TOWARD 2015
A Church Odyssey

TOWARD 2015

A Church Odyssey

Richard Kew
Roger White

COWLEY PUBLICATIONS
Cambridge ✦ Boston
Massachusetts

Library of Congress Cataloging-in-Publication Data:
  Kew, Richard, 1945—
  Toward 2015: a church odyssey / Richard Kew, Roger White
      p.   cm.
  Includes bibliographical references.
  ISBN 1-56101-137-1 (alk. paper) — ISBN 1-56101-136-3 (pbk.: alk. paper)
  1. Episcopal Church. 2. Anglican Communion—United States—Forecasting.
  3. Pastoral theology—Episcopal Church. I. White, Roger J., 1941— . II. Title.
  BX5933.K49   1997
  283'.73'0112—dc20   96-38715
                                                                          CIP

Cynthia Shattuck, editor; Vicki Black, copyeditor and designer.
Cover design by Vicki Black.

Cowley Publications
28 Temple Place
Boston, Massachusetts 02111
1-800-225-1534
http://www.cowley.org/~cowley

Table of Contents

Foreword

*We dedicate this book to those Christian disciples
who are prepared to jump out of the frying pan
of the present into the fire of the future!*

The idea for this book was born as we talked and drove the Blue Ridge Parkway in North Carolina on a very wet April day in 1994. Then it gradually came into being through a series of articles we wrote for *The Living Church* in 1995 and early 1996, reaching its final book form that summer.

Toward 2015: A Church Odyssey is part of a natural progression. In *New Millennium, New Church* we attempted to identify the trends which have been shaping the church. Many readers seemed to find the book helpful, often using it as the basis for adult classes and group studies in their parishes. Two years later, in 1994, we published *Venturing Into the New Millennium*, a small volume that updated the trends and then called Episcopalians to respond to the exciting challenges the future offers. Too often, though, people have asked us, "But *how* do we respond to what's going on?" This question led us to write something a little more practical.

We set out to imagine a best-case scenario of what the church could look like a generation from now, in 2015. We then spell out the radical ways in which we need to respond to all that is going on if we are to take advantage of the opportunities. We have not tried to avoid the problems ahead of us, but we have sought to look at circumstances creatively, not negatively.

This is not a "how to" book, as approaches to ministry are bound to vary from congregation to congregation; rather, this book is intended to nourish parish life. *Toward 2015: A Church*

Odyssey is a springboard designed to help you launch into your future. Although the chapters are part of the larger whole, each can stand on its own and is designed to stimulate ideas and discussion that can move a parish toward creating a fresh vision for action. We have provided questions and study ideas at the end of each chapter for this purpose. We have also added a selection of additional books and publications to which you might wish turn, and a list of resources we believe can help a parish in its ministry.

Toward 2015: A Church Odyssey can be used by individuals, with vestries and outreach committees, and in diocesan and parish long-range planning. It could be the basis for a Sunday morning adult study and discussion, and provides ample "fuel" as we pray for the future God has in mind for us, and as we move into this very new kind of world that is being born.

Scores of people have helped us write this book, and we wish to thank each one, especially those who have shared their ideas either face-to-face, or in response to our articles in *The Living Church*. Futures analysis and vision-casting is not a crowded field in our church, so we are profoundly grateful to those in other traditions whose ideas have nourished us, some of which we have sought to communicate in these pages. Writing a book is a satisfying but time-consuming business. We are thankful to those with whom we work, and our wives and families, for allowing us to escape to our favorite spot on the Atlantic coast to talk, debate, pray, think, and write.

We are especially grateful to David Kalvalage, editor of *The Living Church*, for making it possible for us to float our ideas and receive responses through the pages of his publication. We thank our editors at Cowley Publications, Cynthia Shattuck and Vicki Black, for their input and hard work. Then, thanks to Frank's, our favorite eating place! Finally, we thank God, and commit ourselves to the service of the Kingdom.

PART ONE

A NEW WORLD BEING BORN

Two basic themes thread themselves through the chapters in this book. The first is that the environment in which we are called to be the church is changing rapidly and radically, and that we ignore this reality at our peril. The world that is emerging needs to be understood rather than run away from, while the challenge before the church is how to proclaim to this new world the unchanging gospel.

The second thread is that the organizing principle of tomorrow's church must be the business of mission, witness, and evangelism. The models that have governed our life until now have almost always been the pastoral and therapeutic, the first harking back to our historic roots in the villages of old England and the second reflecting the postwar immersion of both church and society in behavioral theory.

The two realities we identify are forcing us to put much received wisdom back in the hopper, reexamining it at considerable length. The healthy congregation of tomorrow will be a very different place. It will be led differently, the laity will minister differently, and it will organize itself for mission as part of the wider church differently in the days ahead. Whether we like it or not, these are the realities which will shape much of our dreaming and planning in the years after 2001.

The overarching reality, about which we make no apologies for pressing home again and again, is that the world is being reborn before our eyes. Like all human institutions, the church is also being propelled into this emerging age. Business guru Peter Drucker has written:

> Every few hundred years in western history there occurs a sharp transformation. We cross...a divide. Within a few short decades, society rearranges itself—its worldview; its basic values; its social and political structures; its arts; its key institutions. Fifty years later, there is a new world. And the people born then cannot even imagine that world in which their grandparents lived and into which their own parents were born.[1]

Drucker was writing about the implications for business of the post-capitalist age, but he also acknowledges that such a time has profound spiritual implications, requiring very different kinds of churches.

Much spiritual, theological, and intellectual hard work needs to be done if we are to understand what is going on, and to develop the worldviews which will undergird the church's ministry in the days ahead. Bringing clarification out of this foggy murkiness of dynamic change is not something which is going to happen overnight: it will be a long, laborious, but exciting task. We cannot put off doing it—and we should begin now!

---

1. Peter F. Drucker, *Post-Capitalist Society* (New York: Harper Business, 1993), p. 1.

1

A Glimpse into 2015

It has been more than fifty years since C. S. Lewis unwittingly stumbled across the letters that Screwtape wrote to his erring nephew, Wormwood. When Lewis edited and published them, these letters caused quite a stir in the Christian community. Unfortunately, our ability to access primary sources from the future does not compare to his knack of getting hold of leaked information from the Netherworld. However, from the fragmentary bits and pieces of information we have been able to gather, here is a taste of what the future could look like.

Our glimpse into the future begins at a modest suburban house somewhere in the western part of the United States. Barry Donatello-Scott, the bishop of the diocese, and his wife Alicia have just arrived home in the early hours of New Year's Day. Since the turn of the millennium the Donatello-Scotts have celebrated almost every New Year's Eve in church, and this year was no exception.

"How long before you're coming up to bed, honey?" asked Alicia Donatello-Scott, running her fingers through her hair while unsuccessfully suppressing a yawn.

Barry shrugged, "Oh, not too long, dear. There's one or two things I need to get straight before I hit the sack." His wife sighed. She was a morning person, and could never understand how Barry was capable of putting two rational thoughts together after the sun went down, but after thirty years of marriage she had grown used to his foibles, as he had to hers.

Barry Scott and Alicia Donatello had been twentysomething when they first met. Too young to be real Baby Boomers, they were, perhaps, just a little old to belong to Generation X. In their youthful scheme of things, Sunday had less to do with God, and more to do with recovering from Friday and Saturday!

The Scott family were respectable middle class people, but seldom darkened the door of the Baptist church where their membership was lodged. Barry, like his brother and sister, had "graduated" from Sunday school in his teens and then went on to become one of the live wires of the local high school party scene. His parents had worried themselves silly that he might get into drugs, or something worse. Alicia, to the horror of her Italian grandmother, had long since abandoned the Roman Catholic Church by the time she met the man who would become her spouse.

As with so many young couples at that time, Christianity was a nice irrelevancy. They weren't bitterly opposed to it, but they did not really have a lot of time for it, either, and it wasn't until they began planning their wedding that the church entered the equation. Alicia and Barry had ended up at an Episcopal church, thinking it would not make too many demands on them. What they had really wanted was a tasteful setting and good music, yet God overturned their game plan. The early months of their marriage were marked not so much by connubial bliss as by a fearful spiritual struggle which only resolved itself when, one after the other, both finally surrendered to the claims of Jesus Christ.

It seemed only yesterday, in some respects, that their bishop through seminary years had laid hands on Barry's head and made him a priest. Outside the church the sound of military vehicles could be heard rumbling in an apparently endless convoy. He had been ordained on an August Saturday evening in 1990, heavy humidity hanging in the air, barely days after the President had ordered troops from the neighboring base to the Persian Gulf. The peaceful dignity of the service inside the church seemed strangely incongruous with the show of military might outside.

After several years as the assistant priest at a moderately large parish, Barry and his wife, now parents of two children, moved to an unassuming and financially strapped congregation several states further west. One of his mentors, a churchman of the old school, had thought the parish a good stepping-stone for the clerical career he had mapped out in his mind for Barry. Barry had different ideas, and was prepared to stay there the rest of his days if that was what God desired; he had long since realized that "careers in the church" were a thing of the past.

They had been at St. Timothy's just a handful of years, and had weathered some painful storms on the way, when the vestry started debating what would be an appropriate way to celebrate the arrival of the year 2000. Eventually, after months of free-wheeling debate, they settled on a gala dinner at which they could look back lightheartedly on the nineteen-somethings, followed by a service in which they would prepare themselves for the twenty-somethings. They planned to be on their knees in silent prayer when the midnight hour struck. Some had wanted balloons, dancing, and frivolity, but the majority had decided the wisest thing was to be praying at such a solemn moment.

The decision for the service was finally made by the vestry on an August evening in 1999 that reminded Barry of the night of his ordination—except for the absence of army vehicles in the street outside. Most of the vestry and a growing number of members of the still small but increasingly happy parish were already sick of the hysteria, hype, and blatant commercialism that had overtaken this turning of the calendar's page. They felt it right to make plans that were in stark contrast to the celebrations of the secular world.

It turned out to be a momentous occasion at St. Timothy's, and Barry wondered many times after that if the service hadn't been the parish's major spiritual turning point during his tenure as rector. A lot of things seemed to start happening after that—floodgates of blessing, as it were, had been opened.

The parish unanimously decided to repeat the dinner and service the next year when the third millennium really began. This time the dinner was proceeded by a showing of *2001: A Space Odyssey,* and they all giggled at the extraordinary anachronisms in Stanley Kubrick's movie of Arthur C. Clark's book, made way back in the 1960s. The teenagers and Generation Xers in the congregation couldn't understand the ridiculous way the older generations carried on about the film—besides, they were singularly disappointed by the film's primitive "special effects."

New Year's thereafter at St. Timothy's always meant dinner and midnight prayers, and with each passing year the vestry of this growing parish became ever more enthusiastic about it. The first decade of the new millennium was productive: the numbers of new parishioners increased steadily, the lay leadership team Barry had instituted blossomed, and a spiritual depth emerged in the parish. In 2003 they spawned their own mission congregation, which was aimed to reach out to a younger, less churched constituency, and was—to use the jargon of that day—"seeker sensitive."

Then in 2010 the most astonishing event in the Donatello-Scotts' life took place. Against his better judgment, Barry allowed himself to be nominated from the convention floor and was elected bishop of their diocese. By then New Year's Eve at St. Timothy's was so much a part of their lives that each December 31 the Donatello-Scotts would drive sixty miles to join their old friends welcoming in the New Year on their knees. Barry loved going back to St. Timothy's and sitting in the congregation; it was much more fun than the hoopla of his formal episcopal visitations.

As they were driving home this year in the wee hours, Alicia dozed in the passenger seat beside him while Barry pondered his progress as a bishop during the last year. He saw ways in which he was growing into the job—he had even become used to wearing his "hat" in church! He sighed contentedly. Never had there been so exciting a time to serve Christ in his church.

sighed contentedly. Never had there been so exciting a time to serve Christ in his church.

Alicia frowned as her husband disappeared into his study, but she was too tired to protest—besides, she knew it wouldn't do much good. Launching a brand new journal was a New Year's eccentricity of his. Every November or December he would drive her crazy scouring the stores for the right volume in which to record his spiritual journey. As far as she was concerned a book was a book, but for him finding the *right* book was an almost mystical part of the process.

The book would then lie unopened on his desk until they returned from St. Timothy's. Before that, occasionally when she would walk in unannounced she would find him fingering it, as a small boy would the baseball glove he had received for Christmas. Then, no matter how late it was when they got home from St. Timothy's, Barry would always insist on writing at least a few lines. Alicia trudged up the stairs, shaking her head over her husband's compulsiveness and doubting she would be awake when he slid into bed beside her.

Opening the book to the first page, Barry pulled a pen from his pocket, thought for a moment as the nib hung suspended over the shining white paper, then started to write. The arrival of a new year was always a magical, sacred moment to him. A time for a fresh start.

Thursday, January 1, 2015

May I live this year to the glory of God.

Once more Alicia and I renewed our Christian commitment at St. Timothy's. It was good to see old faces, as well as hoards of new ones. As hard as it was to move from St. Tim's a few years ago, it was the right timing. Derek when the parish called a married couple to be co-rectors, but despite my misgivings and some early teething problems, Gloria and Derek are winners. And how clever of the Search Committee to recognize the changing demographics and realize the need for a Spanish-speaker. For someone who is supposed to take mission seriously, I was almost blind to the deepening ethnic diversity of the area.

I think I'm more comfortable as bishop than a year ago. Who would have thought the diocese would choose a priest whose passion was evangelism? Yet this seems to be happening more frequently these days. I'm staggered by the way things are changing in this emerging, metamorphosing church. Oh, we have plenty of fights and they can be ferocious, but I don't miss the old Episcopal Church's "nasty nineties" one bit.

The bishop scribbled a few more sentences, then looked up at an icon of Christ in his little "red corner," an idea he had picked up on one of his visits to Russia, visits which were becoming, happily, more frequent. His meditations finished, he went up to bed. As he climbed the stairs his aching knees made him wish that he hadn't played so many games of football in his youth.

In the days that followed Barry found himself pondering the way that the richness of Christian spirituality from all over the world was being quarried in the new kind of ecclesial body that much of the old Episcopal Church had become.

Tuesday, January 27, 2015

I usually hate it when the weather forces me to abandon plans, but I'm strangely grateful for today's snow. I need to throw off the remnants of the cold our granddaughter, Kate, shared with me, while Alicia is determined to slow me down for a day, convinced I've been overdoing it. If I've been too busy, then what about her? She's always video-conferencing, or flitting round teaching workshops for that consulting business of hers. I'm very proud of her success, but her accusations are a little like the pot calling the kettle black!

Alicia is so into electronic methods of communication that she seems incapable of understanding why I must write my journal in a book and not on my personal assistant. I guess I'm just old-fashioned. To me there is something almost sensuous about the feel of a pen on fine paper, and I need to know that the words are then recorded and I can't change them even if I wanted!

I've also been thinking a great deal about the way change happens. Technology surges forward, and we're starting to grapple with the exciting as well as the frightening implications of the biotech revolution. I'm wondering how much these new biotechnologies and the various genetic breakthroughs will help the human race deal with those resurgent diseases that a generation ago we treated with a few antibiotics. We may be close to finding a cure for the last of the various strains of the HIV virus, but the problems being caused by untreatable severe strains of tuberculosis, malaria, and several varieties of pneumonia are extremely disturbing.

Then, like everyone else, I worry about the ecosphere, and the growing food and water problem that has brought so many countries to their knees. Then there's the economy—it scares me to death that there are so many overpopulated countries whose infrastructures just keep crumbling. I remember reading back in the nineties that the Mediterranean could be filled with flotillas of refugees from Africa. The prediction was right, and the situation there is getting worse and worse. I am grateful that pros-

perity in Latin America has reduced the temptation of so
many to flee northward as economic refugees. Ultimately,
all I'm able to do is live a responsible life and hope and pray
we will find some answers to these horrendous challenges.
If only the older generation who "ran" the world in those
days had realized what damage so many of their short-term
solutions would do, how many would backfire!

The same is true in the church. The nineties were an era of
political games-playing rather than an attempt to see what
God was calling us to be into the future. We did not seem
to realize that we were on the threshold of a kind of new
reformation. We are now playing with cards that were dealt
a generation ago. The decisions of the nineties have become
today's stepping stones, or stumbling blocks.

When I was a young priest I wondered why the older
generation found it so hard to let go of structures that were
no longer working and musty ideas from a passing age. Now
that I'm older myself, I better understand some of the
dynamics of those times and I can see that some pretty good
things were happening, too. At one point, as the spiritual
tide began to rise, everyone was talking about catechesis
and formation. Some folks went beyond talking about it
and actually *did* something. Now we are seeing that where
people took their talk seriously a great garden has begun to
bloom, ripe with vision for mission and evangelism!

I'm grateful that the bishop before me and some of the
clergy in the area that is now this diocese were committed
to the process of catechesis. Especially in some of the
non-geographical dioceses mission and evangelism are *the*
main focus. I have the delight of living with the fruit of
their vision: strong lay leaders, a few visionaries, a battalion
of good givers, some selfless intercessors, a cadre of people
who know the Bible, and so on. Starting formation programs in those days was like planting trees: most of those

who put the seed in the ground are not here to see the results of their labors, but I'm sure their reward is in heaven.

It's exciting to see the rich tapestry of deepening spirituality in so many parishes, although I could get very depressed if I spent a lot of time comparing the healthy parishes with those that are self-absorbed, dying, and often unwilling to admit it. You would have thought that those parishes who see the clergy as their personal chaplains would have died years ago, but they can't go on for much longer—or can they?

The room was warm and stuffy, the bishop had a miserable cough, and he decided he had done enough writing for one day. Two hours later Alicia came in and found him fast asleep on the sofa, a digital recording of Bach's *Double Violin Concerto* playing in the background.

Sunday, April 5, 2015
Easter Sunday

Goodness, I feel tired. Lent has been particularly arduous this year. I'm glad I allowed Alicia to persuade me that we needed to go to the Millers' cabin in the mountains for a few days. So, off we go first thing tomorrow. Who would have thought that little Tommy Miller, the poorest and worst-behaved kid in my first youth group, would not only turn into such a good person but would pop up on my doorstep having made himself such a success in business?

The diocese seems to have had more than its fair share of painful challenges this Lent. Meanwhile we have been praying and preparing to launch an unprecedented number of new congregations. Four new missions in a year seemed like a stretch when we met with those parishes who were laying plans, but on the basis of the information the data-nauts have been cranking out, we had no other option. Now this venture of faith feels right. If all four work, then we will have added sixteen new congregations to the diocesan roster since I became bishop, while only closing down one. Thanks be to God! Meanwhile, it is starting to look as if we might have five or six more next year.

It is especially good to have so many clergy and lay leaders who *want* to think evangelism and church-planting. When Tommy Miller was still a runny-nosed kid, just mention the word "evangelism" to a roomful of Episcopalians and you would have been trampled underfoot as they fled! Today Tommy is one of the most vociferous diocesan voices for evangelism. In fact, he's so enthusiastic about it that at times even I have to slow him down a little.

I just wish I had more priests who shared his passion. While those ordained more recently seem to understand the priceless value of mission and evangelism, the older ones went through seminary at a time when no one was thinking much in those terms at all. When I look at the diversity of approaches to leadership training today, and the offerings which some of our better clergy are logging into all over the world, I wonder that we put up with our "one-size-fits-all" approach to theological education for so long.

What I have found particularly exciting is the things we have done to help identify people with leadership gifts of the Spirit, and then the ways we have called them out, mentored them, and brought them along. It delights me that the rector of one of our healthiest congregations has never been to seminary, yet because Chris is such a habitual learner, has such a healthy spirituality, and has been mentored and trained so well through a whole variety of alternative approaches, he is probably one of the better theologians among the ordained.

He is certainly bonded to his congregation in a way many more are not. When St. Mary Magdalene spawned the Church of Our Savior, they weren't able to provide much funding to help in the birthing process, but it looked as if Chris and Kristen would be okay because of her teaching job. Her difficult pregnancy with the twins put an end to that, so Chris went out and worked stocking shelves at Wal-Mart to keep a roof over their heads and fund his ministry. That commitment, and the prayers which accompanied it, seemed to pay some mysterious dividends in the long-term. Perhaps we should be like those Pentecostals in Brazil who say to a person who presents for ordination, "Go off and plant a congregation of one hundred, then come back and we'll consider it!"

Well, I must turn in. Tomorrow night we'll be sitting by the fire in Tommy's cabin—wonderful! I need this time to sleep, walk the dog, pray, read, and get to know my wife again. She's been so busy: and then she has the audacity to accuse me of being the workaholic!

Those days at the cabin in the mountains seemed to breathe new energy into her husband, and Alicia was delighted to watch him walk their cocker spaniel around the lakes and read for hours. She was also glad that he didn't have much of a clue about electronics because that allowed her to screen the phone calls that reached them in this little hideaway.

Sunday, May 24, 2015
Pentecost Sunday

It's late and Alicia has gone to bed already. I have just finished talking to Andrew Okelu, the missionary sent here several years ago by the Nigerian church. I'm sorry he's going home; we will miss him. Andrew brought with him a true passion for the gospel, and I am delighted to see how his ministry has influenced so many here. I think he showed many of the clergy what it means to be an evangelist as well as a pastor.

The way in which the churches in Africa and other parts of the Two-Thirds World have come to see us as a tough mission field has been something that has really changed in the years since I was ordained. I know I get cynical about the nineties, but perhaps that was one of the best things to come out of that era: a growing realization not only that the whole world was a mission field, but the recognition by the "younger churches" that the West needed reevangelizing. The churches there did us the great favor of not only graciously pointing out our spiritual deficits, but also pitching in and helping us to understand how we could work with God in turning things around.

I will miss Andrew, but we still have Sarah Chung from China, and I hope that during the next few months we will find some others who will "come over to Macedonia" to help us. What excites me about Andrew's return to Africa is the way that so many parishes in the diocese are preparing to build links with the pioneer work he will be doing in a very different culture than this one—presenting the faith to one of the last of the unreached peoples in Burkino Fasso.

The summer was busy in the diocese, but it thrilled Barry to watch the new congregations begin to flourish. It seemed that the Christians who looked to him as leader had at last learned how to get the different stages of church-planting right. The Church of the Nativity, which had grown out of St. Timothy's, had been one of the earliest of the new congregations in the diocese, and the bishop thought ruefully of the pain they experienced and the money they wasted because of their lack of experience.

Monday, September 7, 2015
Labor Day

It has been a beautiful summer. I had been dreading another one of the scorchers we have become used to in recent years because of global warming. At least we can't deny the "greenhouse effect" any longer: the evidence is becoming irrefutable. I find myself wondering what sort of world we are making for our children and grandchildren. This has certainly been a time of spiritual opportunity, but there are just too many crises bubbling, and the climate is one of them. When little Kate comes and sits on my lap and chatters away, I cannot help worrying about the world in her future, a time when I will have already been, as the Salvation Army so beautifully puts it, "promoted to glory."

I am wondering whether to make the environment, the food crisis, and the pressure of population the heart of my episcopal address to the diocese this year. I remember reading an interview with John Stott, the elder statesman of twentieth-century Anglican evangelicalism, about twenty years ago. Even back then he was deploring the way Christians continued in a lifestyle which was inappropriate for a small planet.[2] We didn't listen to him—or others like him—then, but I think we are certainly taking lifestyle issues seriously now that the rest of the world is not letting

---

2. In an interview with Russell Levenson in *The Living Church* on May 5, 1996, when asked what are the great blind spots of the twentieth-century church the Revd. Dr. John R. W. Stott said evangelical Christians in particular but all Christians in general "have been dilatory in expressing concern for the protection of the environment, whereas we should have been first in the field." Likewise, he noted, "world poverty has not yet sufficiently burdened our conscience or affected our economic lifestyle."

us get away with it—nor should they. I am certain the churches are going to have a crucial role to play in helping people to adjust their expectations, and I hope in this diocese we will take a lead.

The year's end seemed to come around very fast, and before the Donatello-Scotts knew it, it was Christmas. Barry had not understood his own parents when they said that the most wonderful thing about being a grandparent was enjoying the kids and then watching them go home. With a baby and two toddlers in the house for Christmas, the Donatello-Scotts were utterly exhausted by the time their son and daughter, with their respective spouses, and their grandchildren left. It had been a memorable holiday, one they would savor in their memories for years to come, but the bishop had forgotten what hard work little ones are! Then it was time for New Year's at St. Timothy's again.

Thursday, December 31, 2015
Afternoon of New Year's Eve

The sky is darkening and another year is almost over. In a little while Alicia and I will be making our regular pilgrimage to St. Tim's for midnight prayers. The parish wants me to say a few words this year, although I would much prefer sitting in the congregation with my wife—something I so seldom get the opportunity to do. I have been casting my eyes back over my old journal to see what has happened this year and how I might lead their meditations into 2016.

It has been an interesting year, and I have been encouraged by the growth, both numerically and spiritually, in the diocese. Over the last fifteen or twenty years people have been more spiritually alert than at almost any time I can remember, but I sense that the window of opportunity could be closing. The Quantum Age has now arrived, and while the world seems to be as unsettled as ever, new paradigms and attitudes are beginning to assert themselves. This new generation doesn't seem as spiritually responsive as their elders, which means that in years to come getting the message of Christ across could be a lot harder.

But the church is in much better shape than when we entered this period of spiritual transition. The nineties got us asking the right questions and since then a reformation has taken place, which means we are sleeker and better equipped both spiritually and organizationally to face the challenges of the post-industrial world. There may be fewer people who call themselves Christians these days, but those who do certainly have a much deeper commitment to their faith than I can ever remember seeing in the church. As people grow older they tend to look back on the past as the golden era, but that is not my instinct at all. While I cannot tell what the future has in store, I am grateful to have been called to be a leader of the church during this exciting period when we have been laying the foundations, literally, for the centuries ahead.

I wonder whether in five hundred years, if the Lord Christ does not return before then, they will look back upon these years as we look back on the first Reformation? By then I, my children, and my grandchildren for many generations will have been gathered with the "angels, archangels, and all the company of heaven"; I wonder whether we will be aware of what goes on here on earth? As my old philosophy of religion professor, an Irishman, used to say, "Ah, Barry, 'tis a mystery!"

2

Changing Worldviews,
Refreshed Theologies

Moving away from a "business as usual" mentality means much more than altering how we do things. There is a tendency for all of us to think far too mechanistically, allowing ourselves to become so enamored by the "how to" of ministry that we completely overlook the fact that our behavior is profoundly influenced by how we think and what we believe. Before we look at the actions that need to be taken if the congregations of the Episcopal Church are to fulfill their potential in the next twenty years, it is vital that we scrutinize the way we think, what we believe, and how we go about creating the intellectual constructs that undergird our ministry.

Everywhere changing circumstances demand that we in the churches reconsider the way we look at the world. We do well to pay attention because the familiar paradigms that have evolved over the centuries and shaped our culture for many generations are in their death throes, while new ones are still struggling to be born. Inevitably, the church's ministry is deeply affected by a society's cultural assumptions, and Christians whose ideas have been profoundly shaped by these prevailing worldviews tend to be skeptical of many of the unique claims of revealed religion.

Lesslie Newbigin, an ecumenical leader and retired bishop of the Church of South India, claims in *The Gospel in a Pluralistic Society* that the culture ushered in by Descartes and Kant rejects "tradition and its authority"; this culture "separates the seen world from the unseen, so that we can only know what appears to our senses, the phenomenal world."[1] This particular approach has profoundly influenced the faith over the years, forcing us to surrender far too much of our Christian distinctiveness.

Wolfhart Pannenberg, one of Germany's leading theologians, raised some fundamental concerns several years ago during a visit to the United States. Toward the end of an extended lecture tour in 1994, he was asked to critique the traditional churches and found himself wondering aloud if they would be around for much longer. He told his listeners that if they no longer resisted nor tried to transform the spirit of the secular culture, these churches were in danger of disappearing.

The Episcopal Church, like many of these older denominations in North America, allowed itself to become dominated by issue-driven thinkers and activists in the 1960s. While the weak social agenda of the immediate postwar period was rightly challenged during those years and to an extent this balance was being redressed, the changed emphasis flung open the doors of Episcopal and many other churches in a different way. Their priorities and denominational agendas were laid open to being reworked by a rapidly secularizing popular culture.

Instead of addressing the changing environment by exploring the ways that the central elements of the Christian faith might be related to the needs and aspirations of modern society, we in the churches allowed our faith to be "modernized." To one observer, we were like a flight of lemmings, eagerly jettisoning "any aspect of the Christian faith which caused people problems—such as the idea of a transcendent God."[2] Not all, by any

---

1. Lesslie Newbigin, *The Gospel in a Pluralistic Society* (London: SPCK, 1989), pp. 18, 39. See also George G. Hunter III, *How to Reach Secular People* (Nashville: Abingdon, 1992), pp. 17-18.

means, were swept along in this flight, but whether we are aware of it or not, most of us have been influenced more deeply by this movement than we care to admit. In many instances, the church's commitment to historic Christianity has all but collapsed.

Yet even as this was happening, the culture was beginning a profound metamorphosis; society's mood was about to enter a period of intense flux. The changes we now witness all around us reflect something far deeper than the ebb and flow every society experiences with the cycle of passing generations. The Christendom which shaped yesterday's church is dead. The residual effects of that Enlightenment thinking still remain, but we are seeing the emergence of radically different worldviews and ways of thinking.

Whether we are aware of it or not, we are at the front end of a massive chapter change of history. The Industrial Age which profoundly shaped our church is passing and a new Information or Quantum Age is arriving. As this transition occurs, unexpected spiritual stirrings are surfacing. We have seen a rediscovery of the soul in the popular culture and a thirst for the divine reordering the whole mental and theological environment. People are persistently asking spiritual questions for which the churches seem to have either mislaid or forgotten the answers. "The challenge," therefore, "is not so much secularization as spiritual pluralism and eclecticism, as people pick and mix a religious framework from any number of sources."[3]

Leander Keck, the dean emeritus of Yale Divinity School, described the churches' plight in the early 1990s in this way:

> The mainline churches have inherited theological wealth sufficient to serve substantial theological fare, but all too often they offer little more than potato skins to those who hunger

---

2.   Alister McGrath, *Evangelicalism and the Future of World Christianity* (London: Hodder and Stoughton, 1994), pp. 90-91.

3.   Graham Clay, "Cultures and Worldviews: 25 Years of Change," in *All Things to All People: Mission Beyond 2000*, ed. Stephen Travis (Nottingham, England: St. John's Theological College, 1995), p. 15.

for a real meal. Indeed, the churches are suffering from theological anorexia themselves.[4]

Major transitions in human history are always fiercely confus-
ing, and this one is no exception. Looking back for a moment to
the last such radical chapter change, the onset of the Renaissance
and Reformation, we see a similar spiritual and psychological
topography. If we scratch beneath the surface of that time half a
millennium ago that we now consider a gloriously creative period,
we quickly realize that the gnawing anxieties nibbling at people's
innards then bear a strong resemblance to those that trouble our
society today.

As the Middle Ages drew to a close, there were signs of deep
and damaging decay in a church which for centuries had tri-
umphed in the secular realm, but had in the process forfeited
much of its soul. New models were desperately needed. The
reformers, therefore, set out to find those models by retracing
their steps and looking for their roots. "The slogan *ad fontes* (back
to the original sources)," writes Alister McGrath, "meant a direct
return to the title-deeds of Christianity—the patristic writers and,
supremely, the Bible....*Ad fontes* was more than a slogan: it was a
lifeline to those who despaired of the state of the late medieval
church."[5] From that intellectual and spiritual groundwork, together with the rise of different styles of social organization, an
unconventional and very different kind of church started to
emerge, one which in the intervening centuries has evolved into
today's kaleidoscope of denominations.

There are more than enough reasons to think that we are
beginning to see a similar restructuring of Christianity. As Loren
Mead writes:

> We are at the front edges of the greatest transformation of the
> church that has occurred for 1600 years. It is by far the greatest

---

4. Leander Keck, *The Church Confident* (Nashville: Abingdon, 1993), pp. 43, 58.
5. Alister McGrath, *Reformation Thought: An Introduction* (Oxford: Basil Blackwell, 1988), pp. 46-47.

change that the church has ever experienced in America; it may eventually make the transformation of the Reformation look like a ripple in a pond.[6]

If this perception is correct, then the sheer size of the intellectual challenge should send us to our knees, to our Bibles, to our libraries, and to intense debate about how the faith's fundamentals interface with today's world. The longer we put off the significant mental "heavy lifting" necessary, the more we are frittering away time and opportunity.

∞ *A Narcissistic Church*

In the Episcopal Church we are afflicted by a certain nearsightedness. Occasional glimmers of perception break in upon us, but for the most part we remain myopic, engrossed in our domestic battles (however important they may seem) at the expense of the bigger picture. We are like artists who, confronted by a huge and daunting canvass, insist on using just a few square inches in the top right hand corner!

As important as issues like liturgy and clerical orders are, we tend to use them as excuses to avoid those vital tasks that stand before us: renewing the Christian mind, providing a solid intellectual and spiritual foundation for tomorrow's ministry. Only when we take up this challenge seriously will we be in a position to play any part in shaping the world that will affect the lives of our children, grandchildren, and the generations who come after them. Our present preoccupations are those of a narcissistic church, focused in upon itself, obstinately clinging to the barren intellectual tools and ideas of yesterday, seemingly incapable of coming to terms with the tremors that have their origins in deep faults in our religious thinking.

You only have to pick up a book like Tony Campolo's *Can the Mainline Denominations Make a Comeback?* to see that Episcopalians

---

6. Loren Mead, *The Once and Future Church* (Washington, D.C.: The Alban Institute, 1991), p. 68.

are not alone in this boat. Campolo's book is a case study of what is happening in the American Baptist Church, but the ecclesiastical profile bears an uncanny resemblance to that of any mainline church, whether Episcopal, Lutheran, Methodist, or Presbyterian.

Nor are the conservative churches immune. David Wells of Gordon-Conwell Theological Seminary has written poignantly of the theological hollowing out of the Protestant evangelical tradition, where substance is being replaced by sentimentality and theology by technique:

> At a single stroke, confession is eviscerated and reflection reduced mainly to thought about one's self. That being the case, the responsibility of seeking to be Christian in the modern world is transformed into a search for what Farley calls a "technology of practice," for techniques with which to expand the Church and master the self that borrow mainly from business management and psychology....Evangelicals are moving ever closer to the point at which they will no longer meaningfully be able to speak of themselves as historic Protestants.[7]

Each of these examples is an illustration of the fact that the entire globe is caught up by unprecedented cultural, social, and spiritual shifts. The mood swings baffling Christians are having the same effect on everyone, from Buddhists to the Ba'hai, from Muslims to moon worshipers. Rules are changing with bewildering rapidity. Those in the church who hold on uncritically to an outdated notion of modernity find themselves forced to embrace unusual and ever more eclectic ideas, from rewriting the historic creeds to wicca services.

We wonder if this eagerness to affirm even some of the most questionable facets of secularity is the result of the unwillingness of "old-line" Christians to let go of the position they once held as arbiters of society's values: they seem to have chosen to endorse

---

7. David F. Wells, *No Place for Truth* (Grand Rapids, MI: Eerdmans, 1993), pp. 101-102.

modernity in order to hold onto intellectual power. But, as Graham Clay has pointed out, this role has played itself out:

> We are now a minority voice in a pluralist culture which distrusts hierarchy and ancient institutions. As a consequence we have to rethink much of our approach to mission. Our circumstances now are similar to those of the New Testament church and to the setting in which the church in India, for example, has functioned throughout its existence.[8]

Some interesting theological realignments are already beginning to take place. Throughout the world, biblical Christianity lived out within the historic continuity of the church is surging ahead, while the traditions which have bowed most deeply to Enlightenment notions and modernity are in decline. Evangelicalism is of growing importance to the worldwide church, including in the traditionally Roman Catholic churches of Latin America, and the Church of England. Evangelicals have no cause for complacency, however; as the heterodoxies of yesterday fade away, new ones are bound to emerge—probably from within the ranks of the most orthodox!

∽ *The Church in a Secular Age*
Our period has been labeled post-modern, post-liberal, post-denominational—post-everything. What all these linguistic scramblings are telling us is that yesterday's world is finished, but at the same time a new era, with its accompanying ideas and intellectual constructions, is still very much *in utero*. Few of the cultural attitudes that will soon be vying to shape minds and win the allegiance of hearts are much beyond the embryonic stage at the moment. The next few decades, however, are likely to be extraordinarily fluid, both intellectually and spiritually, as Christians, adherents of other religions, and the unaffiliated grapple with the implications of these shifts in political, social, and international power. No particular ideology or paradigm will

---

8.   Clay, "Cultures and Worldviews," in *All Things to All People*, p. 16.

dominate, and this fluidity is what makes the opportunity so enormous.

Amidst the confusion there is likely to be a continuing deep spiritual hunger, and more and more people will probably realize that the source of life's true meaning reaches beyond what can be empirically proven or what can be possessed. Those with coherent religious worldviews, who are attempting to address the emerging reality from a firmly rooted foundation, are going to be well placed to offer meaningful alternatives, especially those who are committed to a vigorous historical Christianity.[9] The Christian gospel, rooted in reality and focused on the incarnate and crucified God, is one of the few ideological constructs able to make sense of all human experience and to provide a milieu in which new and strange facts, experiences and theories, can be explored and interpreted. For example, as divisive and disheartening as the debate over human sexuality has been in the churches, the debate has also helped us to look afresh at the relationship between revealed faith and emerging religious pluralism, just as christological controversies fueled the debate for theological clarity in the post-apostolic church, and issues of authority shaped the churches of the Reformation.

How the churches handle themselves in settling both serious and peripheral questions in these years will obviously shape the future. We do not want to repeat the mistakes of the nineteenth-century Anglican evangelicals who were so intent on bringing nascent Anglo-Catholicism to its knees that they completely overlooked the crisis of belief in Victorian England brought by Darwinism and the new science. Enormous energy went into debating the presence of candles on the altar and putting together legal cases like the one against the Bishop of Lincoln of the 1870s, who transgressed a multitude of the rubrics of the 1662 *Book of*

---

9. This case is beautifully argued by Howard A. Snyder of the United Seminary in Dayton, Ohio, in the concluding chapters of his book, *EarthCurrents: The Struggle for the World's Soul* (Nashville: Abingdon, 1995).

Common Prayer when celebrating communion in his own cathedral.

While it is vital that we take seriously the internal and time-consuming responsibilities of being part of the church, we need to recognize that we are unworthy stewards of our time and talents when we allow these household chores to absorb our every waking moment. One of the primary items on the church's agenda in the years leading up to 2015 must be understanding and addressing the emerging theological questions that will shape minds and claim souls for a long time to come.

We are certain that one of the theological keys to the future is fresh study and a clearer understanding of the doctrine of the Trinity, and its extraordinary implications. Perhaps one of the most heartening developments in recent years has been a reawakening of interest in the far-reaching implications of Trinitarian theology, which is the key to understanding both the nature of the incarnation and the nature of the mission to which the incarnate Christ sent us.

Tom Wright, a New Testament theologian and now Dean of Litchfield Cathedral, puts it this way:

> You either embrace this God, this God who is both three and one, or you embrace idols. The first way is the way to life, to the enhancement and ultimate affirmation of the humanness that reflects the Creator himself. The second way is the way to ruin, to the ultimate destruction and dehumanization, at every social and personal level, of that image....Are we to compromise with paganism, to assimilate, to water down the distinctives of Christian faith in order to make it more palatable...?Are we to retreat into dualism, into the ghetto, into a private "spiritual" religion that will assure us of an other-worldly salvation, but which will leave the powers of the present world unchallenged by the Jesus who claims their allegiance? Or are we to worship the God who is Father, Son and Spirit, and to find in that worship a renewed courage, a renewed sense of direction, and a renewed hope for the task?[10]

∞ The Coming Great Awakening

Such intellectual and theological hard work is so essential because it is beginning to look as if God could be lining up the pieces of some great new spiritual renewal. Some are suggesting that a revival is already starting to take place, but we believe such predictions are premature. As a result of the extensive research undertaken by his organization, pollster and pastor George Barna has demonstrated that many of the facets of spiritual quickening which accompany or precede genuine revivals of Christian spirituality cannot yet be found in the life of the churches today. However, Barna notes that polling does bear out a deepening dissatisfaction with the secular, materialistic lifestyle, and a desire for something fuller and richer:

> Our surveys consistently detect a large (and growing) majority of adults who are dissatisfied and are searching for something more meaningful to live for than bigger homes, fatter paychecks, trimmer bodies, more erotic affairs and extended leisure time. Tens of millions of Americans are open to a set of spiritual truths that will set them free from the shackles of worldliness.[11]

Within the churches today we see frustration and despair. "Church" as we have known it no longer seems to work, and appears incapable of communicating the Good News to those who yearn for something more than "the shackles of worldliness." Many even feel that it is the church itself which has been betraying Jesus Christ, confused as it is about him and his call. But the great Dutch ecumenist, W. A. Visser 't Hooft, once wrote of "'the extraordinary capacity for renewal which characterizes the Christian Church,' the way history has repeatedly witnessed

---

10. N. Thomas Wright, *Bringing the Church to the World* (Minneapolis: Bethany House, 1992), pp. 206-207.

11. George Barna, *Evangelism that Works* (Ventura, CA: Regal Books, 1995), p. 22.

'the rebirth of the Church' precisely at those times 'when everything would seem to point to its approaching death.'"[12]

A half millennium ago was just such a time. A Reformation swept Europe, restructuring the churches beyond recognition, and cleansing a Catholic Church and hierarchy that left much to be desired. While the bacchanalian papacy of Alexander VI, the Borgia pope, was scandalizing even the most tolerant of Rome's citizens, a young Augustinian scholar was wrestling with the meaning of Paul's explication of the doctrine of grace and justification in the letter to the Romans. The ringing of that monk's hammer echoed far beyond Wittenberg on that October day in 1517 when he nailed his 95 Theses to the abbey door.[13]

There are enough straws in the wind to suggest that a new reformation is, perhaps, stirring. While no one can be certain of the plans of God the Holy Spirit in the years ahead, it looks as if the third person of the Godhead has something extraordinary in store. Whatever this "something new" is, it will be God-inspired, breathtaking, and integrally part of the business of fulfilling the mission to which we have been called: making Christ known, starting at our doorsteps and going into all the earth.

Could it be that we are edging toward a major movement of the Spirit which has the potential of turning into a great revival? If so, it is vital that we develop strategies to shape the church and its response to the opportunities of the fast-approaching new millennium. A spiritual awakening on a scale of the Reformation will require much more than yet another political game of tinkering with a system that does not work. We are being called to build a brand new kind of church: a church grounded in Christ, fed by the Scriptures, nurtured by the riches of Christian spirituality, informed by fine scholarship, and committed to the age-old

---

12. Quoted by Howard A. Snyder in *EarthCurrents*, p. 302.
13. An entertaining and readable account of the first decades of change during the sixteenth century is to be found in William Manchester's *A World Lit Only By Fire* (Boston: Little Brown, 1992).

mission requiring men and women to be formed by the Lord for selfless service.

Creative strategies, scholarship, spirituality, and the cauldron of conflict will radically alter the church in the coming decades. We would be foolish if we thought the Episcopal Church would come out of this time of transition much the same as it went in. This period of Christian history parallels the Reformation, when within a couple of generations Christendom was transformed almost beyond imagining. The Episcopal Church, as it is now configured, is as much a part of the Enlightenment heritage as any other human institution of our time. It requires radical remodeling. With other Christian traditions in the same boat, we could well be at the front end of a major realignment of denominations—which means we need to be prepared for wrenching, awe-inspiring change. How it all happens is anyone's guess, but we doubt that it will be clean or easy—and there is bound to be the occasional and painful parting of friends.

These events need to be seen as part of a whole new world emerging, challenging the world which is passing—and its intellectual paradigms—for center stage. Our task is to try to understand what is going on, and to see how we can think and pray into it, learning to take advantage of all that is happening, to the glory of God. Now is not a time for paranoia or fear—although facing the unknown is bound to leave us feeling insecure and listless at times. During the next twenty years we are being asked to lay the groundwork not merely for the generation following us, but also for the way the church will think and minister for literally centuries to come, as the two following quotations by two very different authors make clear:

> I believe that America is entering a pivotal moment in its comparatively brief history. We are experiencing the convergence of two significant crises: cultural and spiritual. Without a doubt, these crises are intimately related. In all likelihood, when one of these crises is resolved, the fate of the other will be determined as well. The way we resolve these challenges to

our nation's character and security will complete the redefinition of the United States that began some thirty years ago.[14]

The United States is now entering the third phase of the crisis with the beginning of a sort of cultural showdown. At stake are the authorities and moral assumptions that will prove decisive in shaping the public and private lives of Americans, and thus in determining how America tackles its lengthening list of serious problems.[15]

Clearly, now is the time for bold and sensitive Christians, whose strong hearts are eager to do the bidding of their Master.

Summary

- Our culture is in the midst of a profound metamorphosis, and this is triggering a new reformation.

- We tend to be so engrossed in domestic concerns that we are unable to see the bigger, changing picture that needs to be addressed.

- This is an extraordinarily fluid time both intellectually and spiritually, but it is also a time of deep spiritual hunger.

- Now is a time seriously to reexamine our worldviews, and particularly to seek a fresh understanding of the doctrine of the Trinity, since we could be on the verge of a great spiritual awakening.

- A creative intellectual and spiritual response to the changing world will lay a firm foundation for generations to come.

---

14. Barna, *Evangelism that Works*, p. 19.
15. Os Guinness, *The American Hour* (New York: The Free Press, 1993), p. 4.

QUESTIONS FOR DISCUSSION

- What signs of the movement of the Holy Spirit do you see in the church today?

- What manifestations do you see of the church becoming a minority voice in our culture? How should we respond to this?

- What efforts should we make to turn ourselves into a Christian counterculture?

- What is at the heart of a Christian worldview?

- Can you visualize what a new kind of church, grounded in Christ, fed by the Scriptures, nurtured by the riches of Christian spirituality, informed by fine scholarship, and committed to God's mission, would look like?

- Read carefully through the Nicene Creed and consider how the doctrine of the Trinity speaks to the world that is emerging.

- Do you find yourself anxious about this time of change? What is it that encourages you as you seek to lay the foundations for a new generation?

3

From Deserts to Databases

Before beginning his public ministry, the apostle Paul spent three years in the desert. During that time out of the mainstream of public life, it was vital for him to rework his theology in the light of his encounter with the risen Christ. From the way his theology evolved and the way it shaped his subsequent mission, it is obvious that Paul must have spent days and weeks of agonized grappling with the implications for him and for his future of that Damascus Road meeting with the world-changing Savior.

Once he had grasped the immensity of the message, Paul then went away to work out how to communicate it in a way that made sense to first-century Jews and Gentiles. He puzzled over what he would say and how he would say it so the message would make sense in their lives. Then he probably struggled to devise the best strategy to take the message of the gospel to the ends of the earth. The fruit of those years in the desert is writ large and clear in the book of Acts and in Paul's many epistles. Thinking in twenty-first century terms, you could say that what Paul did while he was in the desert was the "research and development" necessary for effective apostolic ministry in the Roman world.

In today's world, it is local congregations who need to be doing this kind of "research and development." But these days we are more likely to find the information we need to shape our strategies in databases than in deserts. As important as it is to surrender our lives in prayerful service to the Lord and to take necessary time away from the hurly-burly of public life, it is also vital that we grapple with the way the world is changing so that we can speak to it with relevance.

"If it isn't broken," so the old saying goes, "don't fix it." This cautious but good advice worked well in ordinary times, but these are no longer ordinary times. One of the reasons why there has been such a rising crescendo of talk about restructuring the church in the last few years is that increasing numbers of us are prepared to admit that something *is* broken, and that if we don't set about fixing it soon, we are likely to land ourselves in even deeper trouble.

One very healthy assumption at the heart of much of this talk is the realization that the primary building block for mission and Christian witness in an increasingly secular nation must be the local congregation. After far too much time spent focusing far too much attention and far too many resources on centralized denominational structures, at last we are recovering the fundamental truth of Christian mission. *It is the local parish church that is on the front line, and the other structures exist to support it in its work.* The local church is not there to prop up a hierarchy; rather, its task is to be the threshold over which the Christians it has nurtured go out with the transforming message of the gospel into an increasingly hostile and hurting world. As Loren Mead wrote in *The Once and Future Church:*

> In the age of the future church, with the mission frontier close to the local congregation, the flow of resources and attention needs to be reversed. Those in oversight need to shift emotional and functional relations with congregations by 180 degrees. If resources are to flow to the mission frontier, they

must be flowing primarily toward the local congregation, not away from it. That is an enormous change.[1]

Mission is not a tail to be pinned as an afterthought onto the rear-end of the ecclesiastical donkey. From now on *mission must be the central organizing principle of all the local parish is and all it does.* Once this point has been firmly established, then it becomes blatantly obvious that all our structures should be geared to enabling mission: if they are not, we must question whether they have any right to continue existing—and, in the process, devouring increasingly precious resources, time, and talents.

Almost as far back as anyone can remember, this life-giving missionary truth has often been buried—often unwittingly—under all sorts of other agendas. Worthy as some of these agendas may have been, they have not necessarily advanced the church's mission at home or to "the ends of the earth." Even today you can mention Christ's Great Commission in some quarters and be met by a blank stare.

Yet, urged and prodded by writers like Loren Mead, Stanley Hauerwas, and William Willemon, Christians are starting to realize that the Christian culture and society known as Christendom that has shaped our consciousness for so many centuries is gone forever. Secularity has been advancing at an accelerating pace for several hundred years, but in this century, beginning in Europe and spreading across the Atlantic, its impact has been spiritually numbing. As Os Guinness has noted:

> What in most European countries occurred some time ago and is now virtually taken for granted even among European religious believers has been completed in the United States comparatively recently and is still a storm center of controversy.[2]

---

1. Loren Mead, *The Once and Future Church* (Washington, D.C.: The Alban Institute, 1991), p. 55.
2. Os Guinness, *The American Hour* (New York: The Free Press, 1993), p. 66.

The West has been turned back into a mission field, and God has organized us into congregations in order to do business in an emerging environment replete with possibilities. Anglicans in the global South, realizing the spiritual predicament in the West, have already begun focusing their energies in our direction, believing that our churches do not have the capacity to take back lost ground on our own.

If it is to be a missionary unit, the local church cannot carry on as it has in years gone by. Now and into the future, it must radically remake itself in order to respond with the gospel message to a highly fluid culture. At times it might be tempting to insulate ourselves from the environment in which we are placed—or, at the other end of the spectrum, so to absorb the values and sensitivities of this prevailing culture that we are almost indistinct from it. If we respond in either of these ways, however, we condemn ourselves to irrelevance or we surrender those facets of faith which set us apart as believers. The Episcopal Church is always in danger of falling into these traps.

∽ *A Fresh Vision for Mission*

One of the most demanding tasks for lay and ordained leaders alike in the first decades of the new millennium and beyond will be framing a fresh vision and managing the evolution from local churches that are predominantly pastoral, ministering to the needs of their own members, to missionary and evangelistically-oriented parishes. While it is vital that a congregation not remain in the past, it is also necessary that we be sensitive toward those in our midst—both younger and older Christians—who find it almost impossible to adapt to a fast-changing age or to leave nostalgia behind. Some have even suggested that we develop congregations especially geared to meet the needs and challenges of senior citizens. Revolutionary changes require careful and sensitive preparation; even then they are bound to cause profound discomfort for many devout souls. It is the duty of spiritual leaders to minimize their alienation, without compromising advance.

Actually, it may not be senior citizens who find change the most difficult as they adjust for the future. It is entirely possible that those who most adamantly refuse to fit in will be not the elderly, but all those "young fogies" in our midst! One of the characteristics of people in their twenties and early thirties, raised as they have been in an unrooted culture, is a deep need for rootedness. This younger generation of adults warms to things traditional in a way their Baby Boomer parents never did. They seem to have a particular love for the conventional and the formal as they make their way through life, and are likely to protect elements of church life that their elders might want to dispose of. Perhaps they are warning us not to throw out the baby with the bath water.

Much more will be expected of local congregations if they are to be effective in forming disciples who are really capable of living the gospel in this changing world. In the past, congregations have tended to provide religious services for consumers who want to experience them. Moreover, these congregations have been fed by a plethora of programs and formulas, many of which have come down a chain of command from the diocese, the national church, a denominational publishing house, or some other ministry organization with which the parish senses an affinity.

Most churches have tended to be unreflective about how they have put these into practice, doing relatively little to customize the various resources to suit their own environment. Usually, their leaders have asked few questions of this programmed approach to education and mission, but applied it before looking with any depth or care at the particular context in which they minister and preach Christ. Then they wonder why their borrowed approach works less and less well, often seeking to apportion the blame elsewhere.

If this approach were to be continued for a long time into the future, it would be tantamount to congregational suicide. If ministry is to be relevant, hard thinking and careful analysis of both prevailing culture and the local community are as essential as prayer or keeping an honest budget. If a parish is to interact effectively with its milieu, it must not only have a far better grasp of the setting in which it is working—locally, nationally, and globally—but also be prepared to keep taking every facet of its ministry back to the drawing-board as the world around it changes. This means regularly altering and adapting its whole *modus vivendi* and giving up the luxury of saying, "But we've never done it that way before!"

Episcopal parishes are predominantly program-oriented affairs, more prone to producing interested bystanders than forming active and committed disciples. As more and more evidence is coming in, it is becoming clear that program-based churches do not result in "discipled, healthy, Christians."[3] Churches today must ask themselves, "What do we intend to do about forming committed disciples?"

Not only have we handled local ministry in an unreflective, programmed manner, we have also handled global mission with the same colorlessness. Until very recently it was considered perfectly adequate for a congregation to pay its quota to the diocese, which in turn sent its assessment to the Episcopal Church Center in New York, and then to do little or nothing more about global mission. This checkbook approach to ministry meant that once monies reached that central "pot," global mission obligations were taken care of for another year. Parishes could then turn their minds to other things. Paying those dues up the line of command became a test of Episcopal "patriotism," and until very recently even the mildest public criticism of this system was looked at askance.

Our unreflective acceptance of this inadequate and impersonal approach has been nothing short of disastrous: we have bred a church that has almost lost its global ministry consciousness altogether. The words of the Great Commission *must* shape our vision from now on. If we are to be obedient to Christ's commission to take the gospel into all the world, then local congregations must take their global responsibilities fairly and squarely upon

---

3. William Easum, *Dancing with Dinosaurs* (Nashville: Abingdon, 1993), p. 58.

their own shoulders. Leaders who at present have very limited experience and understanding of the complexities of global mission will be expected to plan international ministry in conjunction with other believers around the world. Information and education are, of course, paramount, but beyond that there is a need for a new spirit and a new heart. We have used global mission as an example because it is such a weak area in our own church, but what is true globally is also true in almost every other aspect of Christian discipleship.

Christian pollster George Barna writes, "Ministry in the year 2000 will be as different from ministry in 1980, as ministry in 1980 was from ministry in 1900."[4] He is not exaggerating. The best way to fail at ministry in the future is to try simply to improve on yesterday's successes—successes rooted in a world that is fast disappearing. By and large change takes place as a steady series of incremental shifts which, although they are happening far faster than in the past, are still hardly noticeable day by day.

∞ The Faithful Congregation of the Future

Merely to survive, churches must learn not simply to adjust, but to flourish in the face of this constant procession of transformations. To prosper, they must learn to ride each wave of change, recognizing that the darkest storm clouds may also have the most glorious silver linings. We should be finding out how to anticipate, as far as is possible, what the future holds in store for us; in this way we are less likely to be caught unawares. Any congregation that refuses to accept these realities, embrace change, and modify—or even revolutionize—its approach to ministry in this turbulent period is in for a rude awakening. Such congregations risk emulating the Mom and Pop store on the corner of the street that refuses to face up to the implications of a new Wal-Mart coming in a dozen blocks up the road, or to try to adapt to changing retailing patterns and demands.

---

4. George Barna, *The Frog in the Kettle* (Ventura, CA: Regal Books, 1990), p. 27.

Faithful congregations now and into the future will be those whose primary focus is upon proclaiming Jesus Christ, and living out this transformed life. Such an evangelistic passion will be anchored by a deepening and abiding spirituality. To be effective, however, they must always be working hard to understand the realities of the surrounding culture: observing what is going on, processing what they see, thinking creatively, strategizing accordingly, and learning from what other congregations are doing as they face up to this new set of challenges.

Despite the revolutionary nature of the resurrection message, churches have always had a tendency to protect the institution and be averse to risk. Congregations, when they come under pressure, are tempted to burrow into a cocoon of institutional defensiveness rather than letting their discomfort teach them something about how God is preparing them for some great new adventure. What makes the timid approach so sad is that most churches *do* have access to many of the resources necessary to enable them to adjust to the challenge of the changing world. What is lacking is motivation and courage.

The next two decades are likely to place an incredible demand upon the boldness and imagination of lay and ordained Christians. Old-line, mainline congregations that will prosper in this emerging age will have *begun* making the far-reaching changes necessary, and will be radically altering their direction before the turn of the millennium. Then they will have to be prepared to go on making the necessary and sometimes uncomfortable course corrections that faithfulness to the gospel demands.

∽ The Art of Gathering Data

Congregations need to learn how to use all the data available to them to probe the relationship between the parish and its environment. Data-gathering is not a one-off exercise, or even something to be done every five or ten years: it must be undertaken constantly, and prayerfully. We are not at liberty to alter the substance of the gospel which has been revealed, but we do need to discern what is happening demographically, how the culture is changing, and which social influences are shaping attitudes, so we can interpret the gospel in an appropriate way. As congregations do this they will begin to see how they can most effectively interface with the new world as it emerges.

In the last few years Episcopal churches have suddenly discovered, along with the secular press, that millions of Baby Boomers are on a spiritual search. As wonderful as this is, we should have realized this years ago and attended to their spiritual needs before they began to drop out. Since the 1960s, church attendance has become increasingly "age stratified." Until that decade all age groups attended church with roughly the same frequency. Many of the Baby Boomers who attended church as children and young adults but who dropped out are not returning.

However, by this time we should have starting turning our attention toward Generation X, some of whom are now in their early thirties, and to their children—the first people to reach adulthood in the new millennium. Instead, we find that today younger Xers attend church and involve themselves in formal religious exercises at a lower rate than those who are older, and, like the Baby Boomers, those who drop out are not returning. Patterns for Generation X are not encouraging, especially for the old-line denominations.[5]

For the proclamation of the gospel to be culturally relevant in a time of such rapid transition, each congregation needs to be an inveterate gatherer and processor of information about its world and its immediate environment. Many helpful resources are already available. Churches which retool themselves for effective ministry are going to collect most of their data from outside the Christian community. Only as they analyze that information—everything from new house starts to marketing pro-

---

5. See C. Kirk Hadaway and David A. Roozen, *Rerouting the Protestant Mainstream* (Nashville: Abingdon, 1995). In response to this phenomenon of age stratification, the Diocese of Florida is in the process of establishing its first congregation which is geared specifically to Generation X.

files—will they discover, like Paul, how to proclaim the gospel effectively.

What is there to stop every congregation in the country from establishing a task force to gather and process data? In one form or another, all the information is out there: the problem is uncovering it. Valuable information is to be found in everything from local census returns to national newsletters. On the basis of a tip from a cosmetics trade publication editor, for example, we have made it our practice to read one or two women's magazines on an occasional basis, because often their articles and advertising are excellent early warning signs of changes in the popular culture. These days identifying those signs is greatly facilitated by the ability to plug into the Internet, which is already radically reshaping the culture of our children and our children's children.

Washington, D.C., is replete with think tanks and research centers intent on telling government and business how to be effective in the future. Furthermore, an army of futurist consultants, such as *Megatrends* author John Naisbitt, work with business clients all over the country, helping them to plan for the long term. Tom Sine, a communicant at St. Luke's Episcopal Church in Seattle, does similar work in a Christian and nonprofit setting, consulting with a wide range of parishes and Christian organizations and writing about the future in a perceptive and visionary way.[6] What is to prevent a network of think tanks emerging to serve the churches, anchored in parishes that see the changing world not as something to shrink away from, but instead as a glorious opportunity for mission?

Such a network needs to be independent of whatever formal denominational structures happen to be exist by then, and to have a clear understanding about the task to which the church is committed. Too much of our so-called research in the past has been little more than wishful thinking and speculation.

---

6. Tom Sine's books include *The Mustard Seed Conspiracy* (Dallas: Word Books, 1981), *Wild Hope* (Dallas: Word Books, 1991), and *Cease Fire* (Grand Rapids, MI: Eerdmans, 1995).

A network like this could help congregations and Christian leaders digest everything from polling data gathered by people like the Gallup Organization to the insights of a Martin Marty, a George Barna, or a diverse cadre of futurists, economists, demographers, and marketers. It also requires a strong theological component prepared, among other things, to assess the jungle of technologies into which we have all marched. Above all, it must be rooted in the life of parishes, dioceses, and parochial organizations.

This research and development network would be on the lookout for data on mission opportunities and resources, both globally and nationally; today boundaries between nations have become increasingly porous, even irrelevant. Then as we in the Episcopal Church develop our ministries for the new millennium, we will be asking how these ministries interface with the rest of the Anglican Communion, and, in turn, how Anglicanism relates to the whole of world Christianity—Catholic and Protestant, Pentecostal, Evangelical, and Orthodox—and how we can help one another as we strive to complete the task of making Christ known.

A network like this would soon be in a position to launch early warning flares when something is about to happen that could radically affect the way congregations undertake their ministry. It could also be creating tools, sharing ideas, and providing a framework for parishes, para-parochial organizations, and missionary societies, to know which information is relevant when developing new strategies—and, more important, how others might have used it, and how we, in turn, can utilize it.

Immediately leaders are going to point to the seminaries and say, "Why can't *they* do this?" Theological schools would obviously have a part to play, but we wonder whether theirs would be a major role; the seminaries themselves need to be radically retooled in the days ahead. It is the people on the ground and in the trenches who know the sort of information they need for future success—an effective think tank should be listening to those people and providing that data. Furthermore, it should create the spiritual and devotional environment in which that information could be integrated into the life of the congregation.

For years the church has tended to plan for the future on the basis of hunch, or else be forced to change by pressures beyond its control. The use of intuition is one way of seeking God's guidance for ministry in a new kind of world, and its importance cannot be denied. However, this intuitive thinking needs to be channeled and informed by carefully sifted information if it is to be effective. There is much we can learn about this from "seeker sensitive" congregations like the 15,000-member Willowcreek Church in Barrington, Illinois, even if we have no desire to replicate their style.

This may not be the traditional way the church has worked in the past, but quite honestly, "business as usual" has been paying smaller and smaller dividends in recent years. Common sense should tell us that past strategies should either be abandoned or radically modified. To date the churches have only nodded in the direction of the Information Age: if the church is to be healthy and vital three decades from now, it must learn how to use these resources to advance the kingdom of God. The churches must be forward-looking, imaginative, creative, and in a prayerful way they must be prepared to break out of the worst aspects of their captivity to the past, while retaining the great strengths of their extraordinary heritage.

Summary

- In an increasingly secular world it is more and more obvious that the parish is the primary unit for mission.

- "Business as usual" carried with it the kiss of death. Every congregation must be radically remade if it is to prosper—or even survive.

- Effective congregations are those which are evangelistically-oriented communities of faith.

- If parishes are to be effective they must learn to analyze the prevailing culture, and make frequent adjustments of their mission strategy in response.

- Congregations of old-line denominations, like the Episcopal Church, need to make the most far-reaching changes and course corrections.

- The time has come to develop a network of parish-based, parish-serving "think tanks."

Questions for Discussion

- Fast-forward your imagination into the next century, and attempt to visualize how the congregation to which you belong could look in twenty years. What is your vision for the church in this period of transition?

- What stumbling blocks do you see as your church makes the "spiritual transition" of this new Reformation?

- Read Galatians 1:17-18, Acts 9:26-31, and Acts 11:19-30. What do you think we can learn from Paul's experience "in the desert?"

- What could a "think tank" on mission and ministry do to help you and your congregation enter the twenty-first century?

4

Reengineering Theological Education

With a very different kind of world being born right before our eyes, we would be shortsighted in the extreme if we failed to put every facet of our church's life and organization under the most powerful microscope, asking fundamental and searching questions. Christians are as confused as everyone else at the sight of so many familiar reference points being abandoned as the post-modern era comes sweeping in.

As we have seen already, we are once again coming to terms with the reality that the local congregation *must* always be the foundational way God organizes and sustains people. The congregation is the focus of worship, prayer, pastoral care, and Christian education, as well as the starting point for most evangelism. As change accelerates, soul-searching about the way congregations work (or don't work) grows more intense.

Parishes are now forced to adjust the ways they live their life in Christ according to a rapidly changing environment. Congregations find themselves needing a radically different style of leadership if they are to "prosper" in this different kind of world. Inevitably, as they do this, they start asking some difficult questions of the institutions which prepare the church's ordained leaders, the seminaries.

Tomorrow's leaders, both lay and ordained, face a very different kind of job than the women and men who have guided the church of yesterday and today. While seminaries have to be willing to revamp the way they train the rising generation of leaders, dioceses must also revise the way they identify these future standard bearers and the kind of people they select. If the formation for ministry being offered by seminaries fails to prepare the type of leaders the church needs in the future, then hard questions need to be asked about whether the seminaries should continue to exist as presently constituted. In a nutshell, yesterday's pattern for preparing leaders looks increasingly unsuitable for shaping those of tomorrow.[1]

Yet for now most of our seminaries, in their various ways, still seem to be turning out candidates for ordination based on yesterday's paradigms. The seminaries' understanding of ministry tends to be almost exclusively pastoral and therapeutic; they tend to be conditioned by our inherited structures and approaches to think of the ordained life less as a holy vocation and more as a religious job. By organizing themselves after the graduate school model from the outset, seminaries give future ordained leaders the impression that they are being turned into religious *professionals* who will be stepping onto an ecclesiastical career ladder, and that their particular parish will be "a job site to be abandoned when a better offer comes along."[2] In exasperation, one layperson once exclaimed, "I didn't know the church existed as an employment system for clergy!"[3]

Those who will be exercising their vocation as leaders of the church in the first decades of the next millennium have already

---

1. Both James C. Fenhagen, former dean of the General Theological Seminary, in *Ministry for a New Time* (Washington D.C.: The Alban Institute, 1995), and Loren B. Mead, in *The Once and Future Church* (Washington D.C.: The Alban Institute, 1991), have noted a desperate need for new approaches to theological education, and a new environment in which it should take place.
2. Eugene H. Peterson, *Under the Unpredictable Plant* (Grand Rapids, MI: Eerdmans, 1992), p. 21.
3. Mead, *Once and Future Church*, p. 53.

begun emerging from our seminaries. Many have profound misgivings about the way they have been prepared to cope with the
challenges of today's ministry, or ministry amidst the sea changes
our culture faces in the coming two generations. Uncertainty is
perhaps behind much of the stress, role confusion, and burnout
among the clergy. If the next generation is to be properly equipped
for ministry as the new millennium progresses, then parishes,
dioceses, and theological educators must act now to grasp the
opportunity this new era offers.

In this spiritually hungry and increasingly urban world, satu-
rated by materialism and competing ideologies, tame and suburban notions of ordained leadership are no longer sufficient. In the
years ahead the vocation to Christian leadership will inevitably
be a stormy one, requiring individuals who are prepared to place
themselves and their personal ambitions in the service of the One
who is "servant of all." Tomorrow's leaders must be willing to lead
their people out of the wilderness and plant in their hearts a
passion for God and a willingness to serve God, come what may.
These leaders must be able not only to anticipate change, but to
guide people through it.

∽ *Preparing a New Breed of Leaders*

Yet so much of what passes for preparation for leadership lacks
what the dean emeritus of Yale Divinity School calls the "theological protein" necessary to nourish them for this task. Many
seminaries seem to prefer to remain focused on the past, promot-
ing an education shaped by the tired notions of modernity and
the Enlightenment: scholarship based largely on nineteenth-century rationalist assumptions and at times hostile to orthodox
Christianity in any shape or form, "shut off from much of the
power and pulse of the biblical record."[4] This is no way to train
a generation in the vanguard of those grappling with the challenges of a confused and spiritually hungry Information Age.

---

4.   Howard A. Snyder, *EarthCurrents* (Nashville: Abingdon, 1995), p. 297.

Tomorrow's leaders are unlikely to be the respected figures in their communities that yesterday's clergy were. It will be increasingly inappropriate for them to identify themselves with other professionals like physicians, lawyers, or academics, and they must be prepared to make significant personal sacrifices in ministry.

Even if we have exaggerated the magnitude of the changes ahead—and we do not believe we have—it should be obvious that our educational institutions have a lot of catching up to do. Not only will an ongoing radical overhaul of the curriculum be necessary, we must also be willing to rethink every facet of leadership training and embrace sometimes precarious experimentation. As the seminaries come up against the post-modern reality, risk-taking must become part of their way of life, or they are likely to go the way of the dinosaur. Some seminaries are so heavily endowed that, barring a global economic catastrophe, they could continue on their present course almost indefinitely, but their continued presence will not hinder fresh and imaginative approaches rising from the grassroots. If the latter prove to be effective, they may well take the place of the old seminaries in due course.

Educators in the church by and large are wedded to the notion of incremental change, rather than the major reconstruction of theological education that changing times demand. Tinkering in these times is insufficient. In considering the ways we should think about reordering theological education, we might do well to remember a line written by Lord Tennyson, Queen Victoria's poet laureate: "The shell must break before the bird can fly."

Behind much criticism of our seminaries is the perception by the grassroots that the schools are out of touch with the parishes. Shrewd congregations trying to grapple with today's confusion and position themselves for the future are increasingly frustrated that they do not seem able to find priests who are up to the task ahead of them. This being the case, it is inevitable that congregations will ask probing questions about the sort of job seminaries are doing, as they try dealing with the stresses being placed upon their often ill-equipped clergy. Liturgical correctness is a weak substitute for deep spirituality or evangelistic preaching, pastoral skills or biblical literacy.

∞ A New Way of Calling

However, we would be remiss to lay all the blame at the doors of the seminaries. Seminaries can only work with the candidates for ordination sent to them. While the seminaries have their work cut out for them, diocesan commissions on ministry are also obliged to give themselves an equally radical overhaul. The time has come for them to recover the spirit behind the canonical responsibility given to them for "*determining* present and future needs for ministry in the diocese" and "*recruiting and selecting* people for holy orders" (Canon II, Section 2; our italics).

At the moment, instead of actively recruiting potential leaders, we wait for people to "volunteer" themselves, thus depending on their individual sense of being called to Christian leadership as priests or deacons. Right now it is enough for individuals to say they sense God has given them a vocation to ordained life—a way of life that can look very attractive to committed Christians, especially those in mid-life, when their faith is vibrant but they are seeking a change in their business or personal life. Those tenacious enough to endure the various hurdles put in their path during the screening process are then permitted to go off to seminary. Many who are ordained as a result of this procedure may make wonderful pastors in the old model, but we have to ask, "Are they the best people to lead the church over this cusp of history?"

Clearly, we have turned the selection process on its head. In our excessive regard for individual sense of call, we allow people to present themselves and then, when they have proved they can satisfy the commission on ministry, we move them on toward ordination. However, if we are to attempt to develop a more biblically-based approach to selection for leadership (see Acts 6:1ff.), is it not far more appropriate for the Christian community to seek out and identify those who have gifts for leadership, call them to do the job, and set them apart for that task? Leadership abilities cannot be implanted during three years in a seminary, but they can be recognized, some possibly at an early age, by the believing community—then honed and further developed.

If we returned to this more biblical pattern we would undoubtedly end up with an extraordinarily diverse leadership "corps." We would also find ourselves enfolding the young back into the process. This group has been heavily discriminated against by the church's almost unquestioned assumption that older and life-experienced vocations are preferable to younger ones. We will continue to do ourselves irreparable harm if we go on excluding Generation X from the ranks of the ordained while they are still relatively young. Many of them, raised in troubled times in often troubled homes,[5] are deeply attracted by the richness and rootedness of the Anglican expression, as they seek a believing community able to provide them with practical ways and an appropriate setting in which to live out their faith.

At the moment, if a young Episcopalian is gifted to serve Christ in full-time ministry, he or she is likely to go to a para-church entity like InterVarsity Christian Fellowship or Young Life, and work there among university and high school students. Too often, both now and in the past, because their own church is unwelcoming, these budding leaders have ended up pouring out their considerable talents in the ordained ranks of another Christian tradition. We can ill afford too many of these exports.

∞ *The Great Gulf Between Ideas and Practice*
In 1993-1994 an ecumenical, indepth survey of graduate theological education in a number of states in the western part of the country was undertaken by the Murdoch Charitable Trust.[6] This

---

5. "Born in the 1960s, Atari-wavers (the first cohort of Generation X) lie at the more abandoned, damaged, criticized, alienated end of their generation. These are Coupland's *twentysomething* 'X-ers,' who have suffered the most from the betrayed expectations of a youth world that went from sweet to sour as they approached it. They are also the [generation] most impeded, and angered, by Boomers." (Neil Howe and Bill Strauss, *13th Generation: Abort, Retry, Ignore, Fail?* [New York: Vintage Books, 1993], p. 14.)

investigation came up with a series of disturbing findings which confirmed the perception that seminaries tend to be out of touch with congregations. For example, when asked about their first priority for strengths in their clergy, an overwhelming majority of laity responded that they valued a mature level of spirituality. The preponderance of seminary professors surveyed, however, considered theological knowledge most important, while quality of spiritual life appeared *nowhere* on their list of priorities.

Pastors from a number of denominations were then surveyed. While most were generally satisfied with their own job performance, almost all—regardless of denominational background— were critical of their training, believing themselves to have been "poorly prepared" for the daily round of ordained ministry. Our own conversations with both clergy and laity in the Episcopal Church confirm that a large number of Episcopal priests share the same frustrations as this cross-denominational sample. Perhaps one reason for the perceived inadequacy of seminary training is that those instructing tend, by and large, to have limited experience in parish ministry and even less in the work of evangelism, yet it is for this ministry they are supposedly preparing a majority of their students.

Theological education still normally takes place in a residential setting that either mimics or is closely linked to secular academia. Add the quasi-monastic living arrangements of some, and the seminary is still further separated from the rough-and-tumble of parish life. The result is often a great gulf fixed between the pursuit of interesting theological ideas, and what the liberation theologians called *praxis*—how those ideas work out in practice.

Despite protests to the contrary, learning is seen primarily as the acquisition of information rather than inculcating the ability to think theologically or be formed for the ministering life—which involves laying the foundations for life-long study and exploration

6.   This study was referred to by Timothy C. Morgan and Thomas S. Giles in "Re-Engineering Theological Education," in *Christianity Today* (October 27, 1994).

of ministry's challenges. Given such an academic bias, it is little wonder that seminaries are schizophrenic: on the one hand called to train leaders for ministry in the local church, while on the other dazzling students with the possibilities of endless academic theological speculation. Donald Messer, president of Methodism's Iliff School of Theology in Denver, Colorado, states this dilemma succinctly:

> Seminaries typically experience tension in their relationships with their church constituencies. Theoretically, the church wants to be in touch with the best thinking each generation of intellectuals offers. But feelings fluctuate when these thoughts challenge age old doctrines and dogmas or individual professors take stances contrary to popular and established beliefs. Seminaries officially proclaim they seek to be servants of the church, but the temptation at times to bow and be recognized before the altars of academia may lead to alienation or, at least, an apparent drifting away from the faith community which has established and encouraged their existence.[7]

Moreover, in his "requiem" for American seminaries, Thomas Oden notes that seminary teachers are sometimes looked on with suspicion by many among the laity who rightly feel disconnected from them. More often than not, these professors "are brilliant academics with no experience whatever in the actual practice in the ministry of the Word, Sacrament, and pastoral care."[8]

In all but one seminary in the Episcopal Church, as in their secular counterparts, faculties ferociously defend the tenure system on grounds of academic freedom. We understand the rationale, but the presence of tenured academics with limited parish experience, some with unhelpful theological axes to grind, can, in effect, turn the seminary into an institution obstinately resistant

---

7. Donald E. Messer, *Calling Church and Seminary into the 21st Century* (Nashville: Abingdon, 1995), p. 16.
8. Thomas C. Oden, *Requiem: A Lament in Three Parts* (Nashville: Abingdon, 1995), p. 40.

to change. From the outside, it appears that the whole accreditation process encourages seminaries to acquiesce in the traditional demands of academia to preserve their status as professional graduate schools. For the moment, at least, "tinkering" with the system looks like the only way forward—although one or two experiments now in process could blossom and start forcing some of the changes so desperately needed.

A further shortsightedness within seminaries which may intensify their separation from the parishes is that most seminaries continue to see their primary role as preparing men and women for full-time (and usually ordained) ministry. Despite bold statements and limited efforts to the contrary, most have found it difficult to break away from the notion that their priority is to develop a "priestly caste" rather than discovering how they might educate and prepare the whole people of God for the whole ministry of God.

∝ Asking New Questions

Perhaps one of the most pressing questions to be asked is, how appropriate is it for the academic study of religion to be pursued in precisely the same setting as the one in which we are preparing a new generation of Christian leaders? "It would be helpful if theological seminaries stopped playing at being universities," comments Michael Green, longtime theological educator, former seminary dean, and gifted New Testament scholar.[9] He is asking whether our priority is to prepare a cadre of future leaders with theological specialities or to form them in Christ as pastors, equippers, and evangelists. If the latter, then they should be schooled in the scriptures and, using everything from the church fathers to modern apologetics, be able to think theologically about the pastoral and evangelistic challenges facing a church that is now a body of "resident aliens" on a secular landscape.

---

9. From *Springboard for Faith,* a collection of essays on evangelism and apologetics written by Canon Green and Alister McGrath, principal of Wycliffe Hall (London: Hodder and Stoughton, 1993), p. 169.

Furthermore, the expense of maintaining seminaries in their present style is becoming a burden few can carry. In the United States, the minimum price tag of $25,000 to $30,000 per year to get someone through seminary is a source of growing concern. While some seminaries might have ample scholarship funds, and certain dioceses are extraordinarily generous toward their candidates, the majority of newly-minted clergy leave seminary bearing a heavy debt. Not only does this become a source of intense personal anxiety, but at a time when flexibility should be the name of the game, it usually severely reduces deployment options.

Less affluent parts of the world are already abandoning traditional approaches to theological education because of a lack of funds. For example, the Church of the Province of Tanzania, which is seeing numerical growth beyond the wildest imaginings of most Episcopalians, recently closed down one of its two "classical" seminaries even though the church there is in need of leaders. Increasingly, leadership training in Africa, as in other parts of the world, is being undertaken on an extension basis.

The Church of England is not far behind Tanzania. St. John's Theological College in Nottingham has taken careful note of the way the wind is blowing, and has set in motion a process likely to break the present mold. Far from being an institution in trouble, St. John's has had high enrollments and is arguably one of the more successful seminaries of the Church of England.[10] Nevertheless, as it readies itself for the new century, board, faculty, students, and alumni have been asking a series of searching questions that would have been unthinkable a few years ago.

Among the questions being asked is whether the primary task of the school is to prepare persons for full-time ordained ministry, the job for which it was brought into being one hundred fifty years

---

10. St. John's Theological College, before it migrated to Nottingham in 1970, was the London College of Divinity. It is the *alma mater* of many influential leaders in the Church of England, including Archbishop George L. Carey. It is also Richard Kew's seminary!

ago. Rather than set up false oppositions between training candidates for ordination in a residential setting or doing something else, they have posited a series of questions:

- What if the seminary were to shift its balance and primarily become a resource for parish, crosscultural, and international ministry?
- How would the training of candidates for the priesthood fit in with such a model?
- If the preparation of clergy were adjunct to this primary task, what would the residential module for education look like?

In response to these questions they find themselves wondering if their growing extension program and early forays into long-distance learning should become the primary vehicle for pursuing the mission of theological education, and are already beginning to invest their admittedly limited resources in that direction. John Goldingay, principal of St. John's, considers that it is entirely likely that within a few years the school's extension program could become the financial engine that runs the rest of the seminary's activities.[11]

Meanwhile, St. John's has joined a consortium of schools to form an Open Theological College which could take theological education in an entirely different direction, using the new set of tools that today's technology has made available.[12] Behind most of their explorations is the working assumption that whether leadership is full-time or not, lay or ordained, theological educa-

---

11. These comments were made in private correspondence with Richard Kew.

12. Chris Sugden, Director of Academic Affairs at the Oxford Centre for Mission Studies, points out that "the Association for Theological Education by Extension in India...and Study by Extension for All Nations (SEAN) in Latin America has been the nurturing group for many of those who have pioneered the Open Theological College" (Stephen Travis, ed., *All Things to All People* [Nottingham: St. John's Theological College, 1995], p. 142). This is an interesting example of the manner in which explorations into theological education in the Two-Thirds World are having an impact on churches in the developed world.

tion is a lifelong process. If this is the case, then the offerings they make ought to be geared to serve the needs of all Christians.

Theological educators will counter that while a system of Theological Education by Extension, for example, may work wonderfully in Guatemala, it would hardly be as effective in a complex society like our own. In addition, they continue, while progress is being made in developing a variety of approaches to distance learning, ought we to invest significantly in something which might be able to educate a computer programmer superbly, but may not be capable of delivering the goods when training Christian leaders? These arguments must be taken seriously and suggest that vision for the future of seminaries needs to be tempered by caution, but we should not allow this to sideline the possibilities for major change.

∽ *Training for Evangelism*

Radical change is inevitable, and the sooner we explore the possibilities, the sooner we will find the right way—or, more likely, ways—forward. Just as no parish in America will be able to afford the luxury of a ministry which is bereft of evangelism, neither can a seminary with a venerable tradition cling to patterns of preparation for ministry which are increasingly distant from the startling new world that is being born. Nor should we be wedded to the luxury of using academic theologians who are poorly connected with pastoral realities to train people for ministry.

Elements of seminary life that were formerly sacrosanct need to be reexamined, modified, or even disposed of. For example, is it really necessary for students training for leadership to go to their professors in order to experience the bracing intellectual climate of a seminary? Why could they not be educated for ministry while serving in a parish closer to home, thereby anchoring their understanding of theology in the pastoral and evangelistic climate of the local church? This would certainly minimize family disruption and reduce overheads, but most important it would set what is being learned against the backdrop of day-to-day ministry. If this were to happen, then professors could visit students on site, with their educational experience supplemented by several intense residential courses each year. Such a method would reduce the danger of seminarians chasing fascinating but utterly unrealistic flights of theological fancy—and keep professors' feet more firmly upon the ground.

The Church of the Way in Van Nuys, California, one of the largest Protestant congregations in the United States, has successfully merged the academic with an apprenticeship style of leadership training. Others in the burgeoning nondenominational traditions are seeking to follow suit in some fascinating, creative ways. One experiment in Seattle is a cooperative venture between Fuller Theological Seminary and Regent College in Vancouver to provide theological education in the Puget Sound area; it is overseen by the two schools but taught and mentored by local clergy. All Saints' Episcopal Church, Pawleys Island, and the Diocese of South Carolina are exploring nontraditional possibilities for leadership development and theological education, and have managed to draw two Episcopal seminaries and other bodies into the process. These examples suggest that something *can* be done, but it requires creativity, as well as the willingness to admit that old patterns need revision and to learn from others who are exploring in the same direction.

Not too long ago, an Episcopal seminarian was doing his module of Clinical Pastoral Education in a medical facility in his home state. One day, as a result of a series of conversations, one of the patients he worked with asked him, "Chaplain, how can I give my life to Jesus Christ?" This was an exciting moment, but the seminarian had no idea how to show this person how to make a personal commitment, and needed to turn to someone from an evangelical tradition to help him. In a church like ours, where evangelism has had such a low priority for so long, parish-based theological education would provide myriad opportunities for evangelistic experience and practical training in apologetics, and avoid such embarrassing predicaments.

Greater use of adjunct faculty, which would certainly be possible if more education were parish-based, would enable other skills and disciplines to be interfaced with the fundamental process of learning theology. A seminary cannot employ someone capable of teaching every discipline imaginable, but it could release students into apprenticeship programs which would enable them to gain indepth formation in a particular field—be it urban evangelism or Christian development. An option like this would provide the environment in which the habit of lifelong learning is established. Many others have indicated the need for the churches to be involved in ongoing, post-ordination training for the clergy.

When New Testament scholar and evangelist Michael Green was Professor of Evangelism at Regent College, Vancouver, he insisted that all his students be actively involved in evangelism before they could gain credit toward their degree. Parish-based theological education could make preparation like this normative. There is no reason why a man or woman leaving seminary after three years should not know how to present the gospel to someone else in a meaningful way, and how to help that person over the threshold of faith, whatever theological vocabulary they use to describe this event.

At an evangelism conference in September 1995, Bishop Ben Kwashi from Jos, Nigeria, jumped to his feet and exclaimed, "Degrees from the UK and the USA are not to do with evangelism....The western churches have all the theology and nobody gets saved!" He went on to ask whether it was wise for the Two-Thirds World churches to continue to send their brightest and best to the West for further education, only to have them come back with no evangelistic skills. It is more than an idle suggestion to wonder whether the flow of students should not be reversed—seminaries sending their candidates for ordination for indepth evangelistic training in English-speaking regions of the Two-Thirds World, where exciting ministry is taking place.

It is possible that in the years ahead those Christians who are deepening their understanding of the faith and equipping themselves for ministry will find themselves undertaking modules of long-distance learning offered by Australians, Singaporeans, Indians, Africans, Europeans, Latin Americans, and many others. If, for example, the Open Theological College in England has an offering that meets the needs of an Episcopal priest and the lay leaders of a congregation in, say, Iowa or Idaho, they will bypass the seminaries in this country and go straight to that opportunity via the Internet and the World Wide Web. The challenge to our own seminaries is obvious, but so is the opportunity. If the seminaries here are offering programs that students in Malaysia, China, or Nigeria want to use, then they will garner the revenues related to it. While there is a certain ferocity to the "market," it also means that those who provide the resources that congregations or clergy need will reap the benefits.

SUMMARY

- A different world with different styles of ministry requires different kinds of leadership preparation.

- Ordained ministry is not a "religious job" but a "holy vocation"; tomorrow's leaders must be passionate for God and prepared for self-sacrificial service.

- Restructuring theological education means much more than tinkering with the pieces. Seminaries and commissions on ministry are being called to radical change.

- We should consider returning to more biblical patterns for choosing leaders, calling people out rather than responding to volunteers.

- There is a desperate need to identify and cultivate young vocations to Christian leadership.

- We should seriously consider forming future leaders in parishes rather than academic institutions, because parishes are where they will be called to serve.

- Education by extension to distant places may well be the primary work of the seminaries in the future.

QUESTIONS FOR DISCUSSION

- What gifts and skills are necessary for future leaders in tomorrow's church, both lay and ordained?

- In what areas do you see clergy today to be poorly prepared for parish ministry? What are they trained to do well?

- Study the call of the first deacons in Acts 6:1ff. Could an approach like this be adapted to the twenty-first century? Can you identify other approaches to ministry in Scripture?

- In what ways would seminaries have to change if they were really to become resources for the parishes? What do they do well already?

- What are the advantages and drawbacks of parish-based preparation of ordained ministry and other leadership roles?

- What place should evangelism and apologetics have in tomorrow's theological education curriculum?

- What other challenges do you anticipate as the church looks at new ways to train and equip future leaders?

5

The Emerging Quest for Spirituality

When we were writing *New Millennium, New Church* in the early 1990s, we were pretty certain we could see it coming but we were not one hundred percent sure. We debated long and hard before committing ourselves to a very tentative statement about the emerging quest for spirituality. What we wrote at that time was:

> We expect to see this quiet revolution continue to grow at a grassroots, parish level throughout the remainder of the century. It will fulfill the yearnings of the baptized…to be formed for Christ's service and will become a major theme in the church's life in the coming decade.

Even after we had written this, we wondered whether we might have gone just a little too far.

It was uncharacteristic for either of us to be so timid, which may be why we got it so badly wrong! No sooner had our words been printed than we were being battered from every direction by evidence that this hunger for spirituality had deep roots, and enthusiasm for spirituality continues to grow today. It is far from a passing fad; we would hazard a guess that it is still in the early stages. From a rediscovery of the richness of the Christian monastic spiritual disciplines to the craziest of New Age superstitions, people everywhere are not only rediscovering their souls, they are also learning that these souls need care and feeding. It is beginning to dawn on those raised in the midst of unprecedented affluence that there is more to life's journey than accumulating stocks, bonds, real estate, and the latest electronic "toys." America, which for decades has been on an almost endless Carnival Cruise, is now feeling more than a little jaded, experiencing a nasty hangover, and noticing that its spirit is in dire need of attention.

What we thought might be a quiet revolution has turned into one vast, chaotic, and noisy marketplace which reaches far beyond what could remotely be called Christianity. It is a veritable cavalcade of assorted spiritual ideas. This "revolution" sweeping across America is just one component of a much wider global search for God and for the meaning of life. From Mongolia to Moscow the explosive expansion or renewal of religions as diverse as Buddhism, Islam, and Christianity provides startling evidence of the yearning for the divine among human beings, as they attempt to make sense of a post-modern world.

The press has certainly taken notice of this unexpected turn of events. In 1995, the *New York Times,* not a publication known for its strong sympathy toward the faith dimension in current affairs, carried a long series of articles that provided extensive coverage of the manner in which this spiritual search has led increasing numbers of seekers after faith to explore the offerings of the burgeoning post-denominational megachurches that have mush-roomed all over this country. Meanwhile, faith and spirituality have become lead stories and staples in the national news week-lies, with the faces of everyone from Jesus Christ to an array of other major religious figures regularly gracing their covers.

Evidence of this burgeoning interest in things spiritual is not just limited to churches and the news media. For example, books on spirituality far outsold all other religious titles in 1995, while there was a veritable eruption of titles designed to help people pray. For several weeks in July 1995, no less than twelve of the fifteen nonfiction bestsellers listed in the *New York Times* were, in one form or another, directly related to the spiritual quest—ranging from Thomas More's *Care of the Soul* to Betty Eadey's *Reaching for the Light*. From Wicca to Christian prayer rooms, the number of sites making spiritual offerings of every kind on the World Wide Web continues to multiply at exponential speed. It is obvious that at least during the next two decades the church will be functioning in a more spiritually sensitive environment than in the past.

Perhaps the most fascinating response to this phenomenon has been the surprise of so many church leaders as they struggle to come to terms with this rising tide of spirituality. Prior to the Indianapolis General Convention of 1994, the Executive Council of the Episcopal Church, fearing that they were out of touch with the grassroots, undertook what they called a "listening process." National church staff and members of the council scattered to almost every diocese in the country in an attempt to ascertain priorities. They seemed stunned by the realization that the local churches considered spirituality and Christian formation their number one concern.

These findings were neither freak nor accidental. At about the same time, this passion for and curiosity about spirituality was endorsed by a nationwide survey conducted by Trinity Parish, Wall Street as it sought to position its ministry for the new millennium. Both the professional pollsters and parish leadership were surprised and caught off balance when it became clear spirituality was overwhelmingly the primary interest among respondees. Daniel K. Matthews, rector of Trinity Church, explains it this way:

> What we found through this survey, and by listening to our culture, is that people want to learn how to live a more vibrant spiritual life....They are seeking a spiritually-oriented faith that connects them more fully with the mystery of God, themselves, other people, and the rest of creation.[1]

---

1. Richard Kew and Roger White, "Searching for a Deeper Spiritual Life," in *The*

As a result of their findings, Trinity Parish has made spirituality the primary focus of its life, its publications, and the congregation's grant awards for the foreseeable future.

In his book *Ministry for a New Time,* James C. Fenhagen, former dean of the General Theological Seminary, reaches similar conclusions based on his observation of what is going on in the church around the country. He notes that if spirituality is to develop in a healthy way, then the leadership of the church "needs to draw its primary strength not from without but from within, where a sustained connection has been made with the Christ of whom we speak. Without this our roots wither and we lose that sense of authenticity which is life-giving to others and ourselves as well."[2]

∞ *Spirituality or Self-Help?*

Christian spirituality stands in stark contrast to the self-help, self-care fads that have multiplied during the eighties and early nineties. The huge array of self-help titles that have poured from publishing houses both large and small in recent years is another facet of the yearning for things spiritual. It illustrates our insatiable appetite for a sense of personal completion or wholeness, yet much of what is being written tends to encourage narcissism. Anyone who is not convinced should take a visit to the bookstores that house this genre: the sheer quantity of titles is staggering.

The Christian faith, as millions have discovered down the centuries, does not, like so many self-help philosophies, offer something designed merely to enhance the quality of our lives—along with reduced stress levels and lower blood pressure. The shallowness of such advice is, with due respect to those who offer it, little more than a parody of the new life offered in the gospel, and inevitably fails to satisfy human beings' deepest

---

Living Church (August 6, 1995). This statement was quoted from an article in the *Trinity Parish News.*

2. James C. Fenhagen, *Ministry for a New Time* (Washington, D.C.: The Alban Institute, 1995), p. 110.

longings. Neither does such self-absorption empower for loving service in the way that the gospel does. In this curious time of design-it-yourself spirituality, which mixes and matches elements of the Tao with Native American religious practices in a search for self-fulfillment, there is a stark magnificence to the theology of the cross and resurrection.

Amid this cacophony of spiritual offerings the church is not only belatedly rediscovering the power of its spiritual resources; it is also finding that for spirituality to be healthy, it must always seek to root and ground itself in the person of Jesus Christ. This fact is foundational not only to our very being, but also to our "living": Christ must be the touchstone of all we do and of all we are. Through this continuing encounter with God the believer learns how to relinquish self and is thus empowered as a servant of our Lord.

Gratitude to God for his goodness can motivate our journey and add joy to our service. As the apostle Paul reminds us, dying to self in Christ is the way to both earthly fulfillment and eternal life. The self-emptying ministry and service of our Lord should be the pattern for ministry of each person who claims to be one of his followers. While the self-absorption of our culture will constantly try to tempt us away from rootedness in God, if we give in to these enticements we will eventually find ourselves powerless in the presence of God.

∞ The Small Group Phenomenon

One very noticeable symptom of our decade's spiritual mood is the explosion of small groups all over America—again, this is a topic on which the press has often turned its gaze in recent years. Studies conducted by George H. Gallup, Jr., and Professor Robert Wuthnow of the Princeton Religion Research Center have found that as many as one-third of all Americans belong to some kind of small group.[3] Anywhere from a fifth to a quarter of these groups

---

3. Robert Wuthnow, *Sharing the Journey: Support Groups and America's New Quest for Community* (New York: Free Press, 1994).

are explicitly religious, meeting regularly for Bible study. In the realm of both "secular" and religious spirituality, there is a vast range of small groups, from the multitude of Twelve Step programs for everyone from alcoholics to compulsive overeaters, to gatherings in church parlors and homes for Bible study and prayer.

Although the Twelve Step recovery programs were born in the Episcopal Church and encouraged by the visionary ministry of Sam Shoemaker, rector of Calvary Church, New York, in the 1940s, most parishes do little more than donate meeting space to Alcoholics Anonymous, or one or two of the other programs, rather than see how they can participate in such recovery processes, both pastorally and evangelistically. Yet one knowledgeable observer has suggested that such recovery programs might be the cause of what he calls "the Underground Revival" of the 1990s.[4] Despite their shortcomings, Christians have much to learn from these Twelve Step programs. A Roman Catholic priest, himself a recovering alcoholic, told the relative of one of us that he has found more genuine fellowship in his AA group than he has seen in most churches.

The emergence of small groups of every kind is not a purely American phenomenon, for they are to be found in Christian settings all over the world. The intimacy which they offer can, among other things, be something of a palliative for the loneliness of our increasingly urban world. Some farsighted churches use small groups as the threshold over which people find their way into the Christian fellowship for the first time. Trinity Church in Carrollton, Texas, for example, is one of a handful of Episcopal parishes that have developed their whole ministry around small groups. More than half of those who begin worshiping there come over the small group threshold; they do not come in as a result of the Sunday morning service. The parish has experienced dynamic growth and is a model for other parishes or church plants. For many Anglicans in other parts of the world, small groups have the

---

4. George G. Hunter III, *Church for the Unchurched* (Nashville: Abingdon, 1996), p. 112.

highest priority: almost every congregation in the Diocese of Singapore, for example, uses cell groups as their primary building block.

While in the Episcopal Church small groups have tended to focus primarily on personal spiritual growth, in many countries and in other Christian traditions they are the most effective means of outreach for evangelism. Learning from Anglican pioneers like John Wesley, the founder of Methodism, Christians the world over have shown that there is a need for the intimacy of the cell group as well as magnificent celebrational services and assemblies; when combined, these nurture the faith in extraordinary ways. Congregations from the Diocese of Sabah in Malaysia to Pentecostal churches in Korea have experienced substantial growth as a result of their small group ministries. The notion of the "metachurch," the parish whose whole approach to both mission and pastoral care is transformed by using small groups as the fundamental unit of church life, has been pioneered by Carl George and the Fuller Institute for Church Growth.[5]

Robert Wuthnow contends that the emergence of the small group movement is starting to have a quiet but profound impact upon the whole culture, as it seeks to understand the nature of both community and transcendence. He writes:

> The quest for spirituality is the other objective that has animated much of the small-group movement. A majority of all small-group members say they joined because they wanted to deepen their faith....In a sense, the small-group movement is an extension of the role that organized religion has always played in American society.[6]

Small groups can be intimate, safe settings in which the Almighty God can be encountered and worshiped by searchers

---

5. The Revd. Carl George has written a number of books on metachurch principles, the most recent of which is *The Coming Church Revolution: Empowering Church Leaders for the Future* (Grand Rapids, MI: Fleming Revell, 1994).

6. Wuthnow, *Sharing the Journey*, pp. 6-7.

after truth. Such gatherings will clearly have to be a fundamental tool of healthy congregations as we move into the new millennium. Indeed, Professor Wuthnow points out that small groups flourish not so much where the church is weak, but where it is strong. The tragedy is that so many clergy feel threatened by small groups, afraid that when these cells start to multiply things will start getting out of *their* control.

∽ Resources from the Anglican Tradition

Given the resources of the Episcopal Church and the "goodly heritage" of Anglicanism's spiritual traditions, our church is in a position to make an extraordinary contribution to this global search for the deeper meaning of life. From the late 1950s onward, our spiritual heritage seems to have been treated as a source of embarrassment to many within the church, and has been forced to take a backseat to other agendas. The mood of the times has definitely changed, and far from needing to apologize for the richness of our tradition, there is a groundswell of demand for the gems waiting to be mined afresh—both within the church and beyond.

Several years ago, an organization known as the Cornerstone Project gathered together in South Carolina a group of thinkers and leaders who had an interest in or had made a contribution to the developing spirituality of the church. Their concern was to assess the spiritual health of both congregations and their clergy, and to find ways of enriching them. It is interesting that for the majority of those who were involved in that consultation, a relationship with one of the church's religious orders—St. Margaret's, Society of St. John the Evangelist, Holy Cross—had been life-changing. This illustrates the need for the Episcopal Church not only to continue to draw deeply upon the richness of the Anglican monastic tradition, but also to share this part of our heritage with others outside our communion.

Those gathered by Cornerstone were able to identify a large array of programs and other spiritual resources which were available throughout the Episcopal Church. These included the work of the Anglican Fellowship of Prayer to teach and enable people to pray, various programs of indepth training for spiritual directors, an increased number of clergy and lay facilitators whose primary work is the development of the spiritual life, and the multiplication of everything from spiritual journal workshops to silent and guided retreats. Since that time, we have noticed that there has been a significant increase in the number of presentations being made at major church gatherings about spirituality and the health of the soul, as well as in the positive manner in which they are being received.

The Cornerstone gathering, which began by focusing on the spirituality of the individual, then started asking what the attributes might be of a "whole and holy parish." The resulting wide-ranging study concluded that the following characteristics are likely to be present in such a congregation: a focus on being a *worshiping* community, a recognition that the parish is the place where Christians are *formed* in their beliefs, a desire to be a fellowship that provides *pastoral care* to those outside it as well as to its own members, and the intention to *proclaim Christ* to others in both word and deed, in obedience to God's call. The study also saw a direct correlation between our failure to provide adequate spiritual formation to adults and the young during the last quarter-century or so, and the steady numerical decline in the Episcopal Church, a fate that we share with all the other "old-line" churches.

The Cornerstone Project, as a result of its findings, has developed and tested an offering that has been distributed to all parishes in every diocese, a resource for which the participants realized there was a pent-up demand. This simple method of sharing, reflection, and prayer is easy both to lead and to participate in, and can be used by a wide variety of groups—from bishops meeting with their clergy to vestries and small groups of any kind. By focusing on this style of spirituality at the heart of congregational life, the priority of spiritual growth is raised in our communities and individual lives.

We suspect that the increasingly widespread use of resources like this one will, during the next generation, alter the leadership style and therefore the spiritual life of congregations everywhere. This means that vestries, for example, instead of being purely corporate bodies governing the business of the parish, will share with the clergy in the spiritual nurture of congregations—as is already happening in a number of churches. Where congregations are vital and strong in the way they undertake their mission, usually sometime in the past there has been a significant change in the manner in which the vestry and other leadership groups in the parish function. What has usually happened is that the intentional practice of prayer and spiritual discernment in parish life ceased being just a formality or an "add on" to the vestry meeting, and instead provided the principle around which everything else in the parish's life was built. Prayer is such a high priority of the lay leadership of All Saints' Church, Dale City, Virginia, for example, that almost the only task at their regular vestry meetings is to intercede for the ministry of the parish and its outreach into all the world.

However, it is still troubling that there are so many at every level of leadership who find this rising tide of spirituality, especially a spirituality rooted in Scripture and catholic tradition, alien—almost threatening. These leaders continue to make it a low priority, at precisely the moment when the laity seem most eager to be formed in Christ, in order that they might live out their baptismal promises with increased power. This perhaps provides rationale from our own tradition for the dismaying findings of a recent survey of the unchurched, who when asked why they do not attend church responded by saying among other things that it was easier for them to connect with God elsewhere. Evidently they believed the church offered them little for their spiritual journey.[7]

---

7. *NetFax*, August 8, 1995, from a survey undertaken by Mecklenburg Community Church, near Charlotte, North Carolina.

As we have made clear, the tide has obviously turned. Not only must we pay very careful attention to all that is happening as this current of yearning for spirituality sweeps through our society as we move into the new millennium, we should be doing all in our power to enable those who are now on a search to be found by God, to be rooted and grounded in Christ—rather than looking for satisfaction in the ersatz spirituality of, say, the New Age.

∞ *After the Drought*

The life of the church has always been renewed as it has looked afresh to the way of Christ following a time of spiritual drought—like the one through which we have just come. What people are rediscovering is the importance of being in an intimate relationship with God, where they can be empowered, formed, and equipped for their ministry, and can be concerned for the wholeness of others. As book sales illustrate, in today's world there is a sense in which people crave to know how to pray, how to meditate, how to move into the presence of the Almighty. They often seek after their newfound spiritual life because they see it as a vital ingredient in building stable communities, loving marriages, nurturing homes, and ways to give of themselves.

We recognize that spiritual development is a lifelong journey across the highest peaks and the deepest valleys. This is as true for the church as a whole as it is for the individual. Without spiritual rootedness, churches and people will tend toward a self-centeredness—the what's-in-it-for-me mentality, something we see as one of the major weaknesses of many of the emerging spirituality movements outside the church as well as within it. Our hope is that as men and women are formed in Christ, they will develop the awareness that we are called to be people who live for others. The burden of the church in the next few years is what it has always been, to encourage people to move beyond this innate self-centeredness, from a myopic focus on internal issues to wholehearted and committed discipleship—to be the servants of the Servant of God.

God calls all the baptized to share in the *misseo Dei*, which is to bring to all persons everywhere to salvation through the ministry of evangelization. We do that as we pattern both our lives and our ministries after our Lord. We are called to be re-rooted in God's presence with frequency and regularity, to be formed and to form others for ministry, all so that we can bring the message of hope, the promise of new life in Christ, through the ministry of healing, reconciliation, and wholeness, which is the ministry of Christ.

"The ministry of the Christian," writes James Fenhagen, "is indeed in transition. But where the roots are deep, hope abounds, and the challenges before are seen not as threats, but as signs of God's reign."[8] Sensitivity to this trend must continue to be given the highest priority in every facet of the church's life—in parishes and dioceses, nationally and internationally. Spirituality must make the transition from being the prerogative of a small group of enthusiasts to becoming an essential framework as the church undertakes its ministry in the emerging world.

Summary

- Wherever you look in the world, and especially in the United States, there is a growing hunger after and enthusiasm for the development of personal spirituality.

- Surveys have suggested developing spirituality has to be a number one priority of the churches in the future.

- Christian spirituality is not built around self-absorption and self-help, but begins at Christ's cross and resurrection and calls for self-emptying and selfless vocation.

---

8. Fenhagen, *Ministry for a New Time*, p. 123.

- Where the church is strong small groups flourish. Small groups are an "underground revival."

- Anglicanism has "a goodly heritage" of spiritual traditions to offer and on which to draw.

- In-house resistance to spirituality can often be high, especially from leaders who feel threatened.

QUESTIONS FOR DISCUSSION

- Look at the world around you and attempt to identify manifestations of the quest for spirituality in the lives of people you know, as well as in businesses and organizations in your own locality.

- What role do small groups play in your parish? If the role they play is insignificant, what is the reason for this? What do you think you should do about it?

- In what ways does your vestry model the importance of being grounded in God? How does it provide for spiritual growth for your congregation?

- How do you see the church helping its members move from self-centeredness and self-absorption to self-emptying discipleship?

- Beginning with Philippians 2:5-11, what does the Bible say about "self-emptying" for the Christian?

- Read Jeremiah 1:1-10 and discuss the ways in which God challenges us to the limit of our resources and beyond. How are divine resources provided to discharge our call?

PART TWO

A New Apostolic Age

Over and over again during the last few years, we have said to audiences in all corners of the church that this is probably the most exciting time in history to be a Christian. All too often we are greeted by blank stares, or "Yes, but...." It is an exciting time for the church because the new world that is being born, despite all the question marks which hang over it, shows every sign of being a new "apostolic age."

The crumbling of the secular mindset, with its roots in the Enlightenment, has opened doors that just a few years ago appeared to have been slammed shut in our faces. It seemed then that those of us who believe life has a spiritual dimension were being relegated permanently to the margins of the culture, and treated as if we were simple-minded or just plain stupid. The church's response was either to attempt to baptize the secular agenda in a desperate effort to retain our position as the arbiters of the culture, or to accustom "ourselves to an obscure life in the shadow of arrogant Rationalism and bullying Technology."[1]

The floodtide which each day is sweeping aside the remnants of rationalism, the residue of the Enlightenment, is altering people's perceptions of reality. New veins of opportunity are being

---

1. Eugene H. Peterson, "Spirit Quest," in *Christianity Today* (November 8, 1993), pp. 27-28.

uncovered, waiting to be mined by the churches—if they have the
eyes to see them. The Christian movement today faces more
exciting possibilities for life-changing, world-transforming mission than at any time in the history of the United States of
America. Eugene Peterson comments:

> People all around us—neighbors and strangers, rich and poor,
> Communists and capitalists—want to know about God. They
> ask questions about meaning and purpose, right and wrong,
> heaven and hell....Instead of plotting ways that we can get
> people interested in God, they are calling us up, pulling on our
> sleeves, asking: "We would see Jesus." They, of course, do not
> always (not even often) say Jesus. But they have had it with
> the world and their lives the way they are, and they have the
> good sense to realize that improved goods and services are not
> going to help.[2]

Perhaps the reason that so few respond to mission endeavors
is that our vision for the heart of the church's mission and
evangelism has faltered. In reality, we have ceased to be an
ekklesia—that is, a community of people called into being by God
in order to be equipped to go out into the world bearing the Good
News of the cross and resurrection. Instead, we are better char-
acterized as comprising a network of chaplaincies who "do
church" in the same way we have always done it on a Sunday
morning—but for an ever-dwindling constituency. The urge is to
preserve the institution, rather than to respond to the call of God.

We must discover how to preserve the riches of our legacy of
fifteen hundred years of Christendom, but we must also learn how
to remodel this heritage so that it cuts ice in a much a sterner age.
Growing numbers of the unchurched in our communities instinc-
tively know they are in spiritual trouble but have no idea of where
to look for help. Their interest in Buddhism or New Age, medieval
chant or environmental crusades, writes George Hunter, "is a sign
of receptivity and an active seeking for ultimate reality. Jesus had

---

2. *Ibid.*

to coach his first followers, 'Look around you and see how the fields are ripe for the harvesting' (John 4:35)....The churches today that perceive a receptive mission field, and engage in it appropriately, are gathering great harvests."[3]

The second part of this book will focus on this missionary ministry to which God has called us. We can talk until we are blue in the face about decisions of General Conventions, about who has or who hasn't been elected bishop, or chew for hours over the latest piece of gossip to be churned out by the ecclesiastical rumor mills, but if we are not prayerfully engaged in the mission of witness and evangelism, the *misseo Dei,* then, as Archbishop George Carey recently noted, we may well have surrendered the right to be called a church at all.[4]

---

3. George G. Hunter III, *Church for the Unchurched* (Nashville, Abingdon, 1996), p. 21.

4. The Archbishop of Canterbury mentioned this idea in an aside in his opening address to the Global Conference for Dynamic Evangelism into the Twenty-first Century at Kanuga in September 1995.

6

Putting Evangelism First

E vangelism is the primary passport to a healthy future, whether Episcopalians like it or not. Yet, as we pointed out several years ago in *New Millennium, New Church*, many of us not only suffer from "evangelism phobia," we even boast of how uncomfortable it makes us! There is the strange and abiding perception in our midst that evangelism is the domain of fundamentalists or "renewal people," and people in churches like ours should not dabble in it.

Perhaps we find it difficult to identify with those who appear to do the most talking about evangelism. Often they are Christians who insist on wearing their hearts on the sleeves, and that isn't our style. However, you might be surprised exactly *who* is talking more and more about evangelism these days. Pope John Paul II, for example, has told Roman Catholics that "proclamation is the permanent priority of mission," and making Christ known is the church's reason for existing. Patriarch Alexy II of Moscow claims that "the most urgent task...of the entire church is a ministry of intense evangelization aimed at filling the enormous spiritual vacuum."[5] Meanwhile, the Archbishop of Canterbury is making precisely the same affirmation: "Evangelism is not incidental to the life of the church, it is fundamental to it. A church

---

5. Quoted in *Christianity Today* (June 19, 1995).

which does not engage in God's work of reconciliation is simply a disobedient church."[6]

So we say it again: *evangelism is the primary passport to a healthy future.* When a parish rediscovers its passion for evangelism, every facet of that congregation's life is ignited. Worship is revitalized, the Bible comes alive, spirituality is enriched, stewardship turns from "tipping God" to making a sacrifice, and the quality of Christian education for all ages soars. Pastoral care, far from being neglected, almost always improves. All these factors working together spill outward in a great flood of selfless service. As the mid-century theologian Emil Brunner put it, "The church lives by mission as a fire lives by burning." In this post-modern, post-Christian, post-everything age, loving, caring, sensitive outreach and evangelism are at the root of congregational health. Sensitivity is, perhaps, the key. If we ourselves are unhappy about certain approaches to sharing our faith, such approaches will probably elicit the same response in those to whom we take the message.

Everywhere people are realizing there is more to life than climbing the social ladder. A recent commentator has suggested that Americans "are by nature a busy and ambitious people whom tectonic social forces—declining average wage, high rate of divorce, two-paycheck families, instant telecommunications, jet travel across time zones, growing popularity of soccer for everyone older than four—have turned into a race of laboratory rats on a treadmill going nowhere fast."[7] Amid so much disorientation, people are yearning ever more deeply for something that fills the spiritual void and provides a perspective on the world that will help them to start making sense of changing realities.

Eras of transition are not easy times in which to live, but during such times those outside the Christian faith are often more ready

---

6. The Most Revd. George L. Carey, in his opening address to the Global Conference for Dynamic Evangelism into the Twenty-first Century, Kanuga, September 1995.

7. Michael J. Sandel, in *The Atlantic Monthly* (March 1996).

to listen to the gospel. Perhaps it is because the orderliness of yesterday is gone, and people are searching for new answers. Bill Easum has described times of transition in this way:

> Things in the environment that disturb a system's equilibrium help create new forms of order. Chaos or disorder become the source of new order instead of something to be avoided. Chaos is desirable because it is the start of something new.[8]

In this age of transition one of the fundamental factors we have to take into account is that people are less likely than ever before to go out looking for answers at a church; indeed, the church could very well be the last place they look. It is conceivable they will be drawn to any number of religious groups, or to one of the many emerging "secular spiritualities." However, the accumulating evidence suggests that seekers *are* drawn into Christian communities when those churches are visionary, present the faith sensitively but without apology, and where visitors are treated as people whose potential will not be fully revealed until they are found by Jesus Christ.

In the United States today people are not unresponsive to the message of the gospel; quite to the contrary. The problem is that most Episcopal parishes have not "plugged into" the rich veins of possibility, and are often blind to the opportunities on their own doorsteps. While such parishes are becalmed, dynamic new churches have sprung up and been extraordinarily effective reaching the unchurched in precisely the same neighborhoods. Frequently, the only way Episcopalians and the other traditional churches have been able to deal with the "threat" of the burgeoning post-denominational community church down the block is to criticize or belittle that congregation's inevitable shortcomings, rather than asking what we can learn from them. Their wholehearted commitment to the mission of the church usually puts us

---

8. William Easum, *Sacred Cows Make Gourmet Burgers* (Nashville: Abingdon, 1995), p. 25.

to shame, even if we are not particularly attracted to their ministry style and have no wish to emulate it.

Some have criticized our enthusiasm for evangelism and mission, asking whether we want to abandon or sacrifice the best of the ancient spiritual disciplines and sacramental patterns of life that nourished our forebears. Yet we are convinced that these age-old Anglican patterns of devotion and discipline, far from being diminished by a reorientation of the church toward outreach, will in fact be revitalized by it. We are not suggesting *either/or*, but *both/and*. Anglicans have a remarkable set of resources at their disposal, and they provide the spiritual undergirding for fresh missionary advances and much more. The task ahead is to direct these energies away from self-absorption and toward mission.

∞ *The Urge to Plant Churches*
When many congregations engage in gospel outreach, their primary reason for doing so—whether that reason is spoken or not—is usually survival. This vision is too small. Truly apostolic communities, those with a passion for evangelism, are parishes whose strategy is rooted and grounded in obedience to the risen Jesus Christ whose final words to his disciples were the Great Commission, sending them out to make disciples of all nations (see Matthew 28:16-19). Great Commission congregations are concerned not only with those on their doorstep, but long to play a part in taking the gospel message to those who have never heard it. It is our observation that healthy congregations are not only evangelistic, but also globally-minded and deeply involved in ministries of care to those in need.

It is usually such congregations who see the "fields ripe for harvest" in their own vicinity, and set about launching new congregations patterned in such a way that they are able to reach these unchurched ones. They make sure that new mission congregations are planted in appropriate environments, and are geared to reach out in culturally relevant ways. Planting new congregations is the very best way to bring the message of Christ to a fresh network of people; they are also likely to be the settings in which exciting new approaches to mission and ministry can be explored. While many attempted church-plants, like new businesses, go under, the statistics show that new congregations, when properly nurtured, have the best potential for numerical growth.

In the first ninety days of its existence, for example, the Episcopal Church on the Square, Lady Lake, Florida, gathered a worshiping congregation of over two hundred people. What makes their case particularly unusual is that the new church is set in a retirement area, and many of its members had little or no church involvement prior to settling in Florida: clearly, it is not only the young who are spiritually restless. Peter Wagner, a scholar of healthy church life, has suggested that there are bountiful opportunities in the many retirement communities in the south and southwest that are filled with senior citizens from whose lives the gospel is missing.

The Church of the Word in Gainesville, Virginia, is entirely different from Lady Lake. When Alison Barfoot became vicar of this struggling church plant of five families in 1990, it looked as if the plant had not taken root. Reading between the lines, she wondered whether the bishop had sent her there in order to give the congregation one last chance, or to bring a decent Christian burial to the mission. Today the church is housed in a blue-porched building that was once a plant nursery, and is geared to reach the growing number of people in their twenties and thirties who are moving into the area. Unashamedly "renewed" in its style, a skilled band and singing ensemble lead the worship, and the words of the liturgy are projected onto a large screen to one side of the altar by an overhead projector. What is interesting is that the Church of the Word is only a few minutes' drive from another, far more traditional Episcopal parish, illustrating how new congregations can be established in close proximity to more settled parishes and draw an entirely different constituency.

Participants in the Shaping Our Future symposium, which was held in St. Louis several years ago to look at the future of Episcopal organizational structures, soon discovered that the most effective way to revitalize the church is not through church councils and conventions, but by sharing the faith and planting new missions. The lasting fruit of that gathering on the banks of the flood-swollen Mississippi in the soggy summer of 1993 is likely to be NAMS—the North American Missionary Society—whose mission is to enable effective church-planting here at home. While it is too early to see where this ministry will go under the leadership of the Revd. Jon Shuler, a number of new initiatives are currently underway as a result of its work, and at the very least planting new congregations has been moved higher on the church's agenda in many places.

Neither is it an accident that when it comes to launching new congregations, the liveliest dioceses are not necessarily those with a long pedigree and great endowment, but those whose commitment to mission is eager and strong. Indeed, the "establishment" is most often not the place to look for exciting new initiatives and new ideas. Bill Easum, a United Methodist pastor, points out that the people who grasp the opportunities on this hinge of history are "fringe people" who are "willing to concentrate on the opportunities rather than the threats."[9]

New congregations planted in recent years are seldom clones of the traditional Episcopal parish of yesteryear, but a fascinating mix of styles and target populations. Christ Church in Albertville, Alabama, saw a possible mission field among the ten thousand Spanish-speakers in their county who work in chicken-processing plants or at a huge outlet mall, and who were not being reached by anyone else, Protestant or Roman Catholic. Today that little parish on Sand Mountain, some sixty miles north of Birmingham, is home to a second congregation that is Hispanic, growing, and dynamic. When properly launched, many new congregations resemble the Church of the Holy Spirit in El Paso, Texas, which has grown so fast that its building program cannot keep up with exploding numbers.

---

9. William Easum, *Dancing with Dinosaurs* (Nashville: Abingdon, 1993), p. 37.

While we might not be on target for planting one thousand new congregations in the Decade of Evangelism—a goal set by General Convention in 1991—the Episcopal Church is at long last putting together new churches more creatively than at any time in recent history. Formerly quiescent dioceses are starting to redeploy their resources to make use of these opportunities, exploring creative strategies to get the gospel message out. For example, a number of dioceses, rather than indefinitely subsidizing missions, are diverting funds to new congregations and investing in growth opportunities. The lessons from these new church-plants need to be learned—and enthusiastically embraced—by the whole Episcopal Church if it is to have a healthy future.

While some basic principles for effectively planting new churches have been developed, there is no one particular model for success. New congregations can be charismatic, evangelical, or even very traditional—as long as their primary focus is upon the lordship of Jesus Christ and the spread of the gospel. In a world craving for rootedness, our rich Anglican heritage as it is adapted to the changing environment, is a potent calling card in the life of new congregations.

∞ Learning from Other Denominations

Successful church-plants have to be more than simply part of a coherent strategy. They need good planning, lots of prayer, and adequate preparation, as well as a supply of good information. Venturing forth in faith is suicidal if the necessary homework has not been done beforehand. This is one of the secrets behind the rapid expansion of the conservative denomination called the Church of the Nazarene. Good data is so important to its leaders that they have set up a small unit in their Kansas City seminary to process and provide the information they need. Such foresight is evidence that the Nazarenes are not waiting for the great sea change of post-modernity to sweep over them, but are already making plans for the twenty-first century.

One of the tasks of the Nazarenes' church-planting unit is to examine demographic and other kinds of data which will give them an idea of the communities where potential church members are going to settle and where they might get their local congregations to start focusing their attention. Other churches are also making use of such data: the Episcopal Diocese of West Missouri, for example, is availing itself of this resource in its own area. Others still are making use of information which can be purchased at modest prices from a variety of sources.

The Church of the Redeemer, Jacksonville, Florida, is one Episcopal congregation that is discovering how important information is to church planting. Established in a suburb to the south of the city some twenty years ago, the Redeemer finds itself in the middle of a huge development of rental apartments and condos. By culling the Internet and other sources of data, they now have a pretty good statistical picture of their zip code area and are creating a strategy to take Christ's message into these transient housing complexes of mostly single people. Part of this strategy involves parishioners moving into apartments in these complexes and becoming little "colonies of heaven" in the middle of the lonely isolation. The leadership of this parish is also playing a part in the plans of the Diocese of Florida to launch a generational congregation whose sole mission is to reach out to Generation X and their children.

Few Episcopal dioceses demonstrate such foresight, even though failing to develop such a vision has consequences that may be catastrophic. Our tendency has been to play the hunch, and more often than not hunches have a habit of going badly wrong. We must get beyond being amateurs at church-planting. It is vital that our seminaries, whatever form they are going to take in the future, play a major role training a generation of Christian leaders, both lay and ordained, who relish the opportunity to establish dynamic new congregations. One encouraging sign is the plan of Seabury-Western Theological Seminary to offer a doctorate in congregational development. Many more hands-on training opportunities like this are vital for both lay as well as ordained leaders.

This is not the time to become insular. We have a lot to learn from the Nazarenes as well as from organizations like the Christian and Missionary Alliance. In Latin America this group has pursued what it calls the Encounter With God strategy. This has been extremely successful during its twenty-five years, and the strategy is now being used in a number of countries, including among Spanish-speakers in the Miami, Florida, area. Beginning with Lima, Peru, the strategy has enabled the founding organization to establish several dozen thousand-member churches, while new congregations with similar targets for membership are being born all the time. It is interesting to make a comparison with Anglican church-plants that began in Peru at the same time using more traditional methods. The Anglican Diocese of Peru has been encouraged by its progress, but its membership is only one-tenth of the number (35,000 or more) who worship in Christian and Missionary Alliance congregations, yet they are ministering in similar areas and among similar social groups.

The Encounter With God approach to church-planting is now being tested in an Anglican setting in the Diocese of Honduras. After three years, the Church of Cristo Redentor, Tegucigalpa, has a worshiping congregation that numbers over two hundred, is continuing to grow, and is well on the way to becoming a thousand-member congregation by the turn of the millennium. It is already the largest contributor to the diocese. Its goal is to be self-sufficient and to plant daughter congregations bearing the same evangelistic make-up and growing to the same size. At the heart of the strategy is the notion that a new church is not considered a success when it has finally paid off its mortgage and has a full-time priest, but starts succeeding only when it has managed to plant a daughter church also able to reproduce itself.

We see no reason why this strategy, properly adapted, should not be tried all over the United States by Episcopalians eager to share the gospel of Christ Jesus with their friends and neighbors. The principles are good, and the secret of good missionary work is not slavishly copying what someone else has done, but being able to adapt principles to apply the changeless message of the gospel in a variety of cultural, ethnic, or sociological settings.

Hearts beat faster and creative juices flow more freely when we envision the diocese of the future as one whose commitment to evangelism has enabled it to give rise to two, three, or more thousand-member parishes in the next few decades, all of which are reproducing themselves and are helping out with the ministries of those congregations which, because of location or other circumstances, do not have the same growth potential. Parishes planted in this way, certainly in the first generation or two, would not be congregations who sit back and pat themselves on the back about their lovely buildings and beautiful pipe-organs, but would be congregations planning, praying, and looking toward their next church-plant.

Some complain that congregations like these are obsessed with numbers to the exclusion of everything else: that they are nothing more than sophisticated "scalp-hunting" operations. This is far from true. Encounter With God congregations have demonstrated a heightened social consciousness, something already being displayed in embryonic form in Cristo Redentor, Tegucigalpa. Their vision is to develop congregational ministry that reaches out in a whole variety of ways to the whole person. Those who find fault with these planned approaches to evangelism and outreach are very often those whose own ministry is likely to be shrinking: a ministry that does not grow but instead shrinks thirty or forty percent in a decade or two is by its very nature having to spend proportionately more of its funds keeping the institution afloat, rather than doing to work to which it is supposed to be committed.[10]

Those churches which grow and flourish in the future will not be those whose primary goal is to establish an unbeatable music ministry or support a successful soup kitchen, worthy and impor-

---

10. The statistics from many dioceses which have not taken evangelism seriously and have majored in being "prophetic" are sobering in the extreme, registering huge loses of membership—and therefore, donors. Projected outward to 2015, it is likely some of them will have ceased to exist altogether if they are not able to turn themselves around.

tant as such things are. Rather, they will increasingly be the ones who have learned the lesson that Christian growth only comes when you are committed to giving away your faith. Soup kitchens, outstanding music programs, and ministry to those living with AIDS are the natural *by-products* of visionary evangelism, but they are not the primary goal.

If we continue to model our churches on our nostalgic ideas of the self-contained bucolic English parish of the past, then we can say good-bye not only to individual congregations, but also to large chunks of what remains of the Episcopal Church. Parishes and dioceses working together have no option but to develop long-range and faithful strategies to bring people to Christ. At the heart of such strategies will be the birthing of new congregations, and those who do not embrace these or similar strategies will continue to dwindle both numerically and financially, and will ultimately shrivel away completely. Already in certain parts of the country we can see this decline happening.

Church-planting is a challenge to be embraced with great enthusiasm if dioceses of the Episcopal Church are to be players in the ongoing spiritual journey of this nation and the world. Refusal to grapple with it is a decision not just to be "also-rans," but more likely "has-beens." The Episcopal Church does not have a divine right to exist. Only as we rediscover our divine purpose for being will God honor and bless us.

∽ Churches Can Die

A few years ago, one of us was being driven to a meeting through the rolling countryside of upstate New York. Meandering through a pretty little country town, the retired priest who was traveling with us sighed, "We used to have a thriving Episcopal church here." As we passed the end of the street, he pointed to where the building had once been situated, and he told the depressing, but familiar, story of its decline and demise. It was a story that could be repeated a thousand times over—indeed, at this very minute there are churches of every denomination dying all over this land.

While the Ayatollah Khomeni may have ordered the buildings of St. Paul's Anglican Church in Teheran bulldozed to the ground and the congregation scattered during the Islamic Revolution in that country in the late 1970s, churches in the United States are seldom forced out of business so violently. Usually it is congregations themselves who decide whether or not they are going to live or die. The day on which the doors close, the windows are boarded up, and the sign is taken down is the final scene of the last act of a series of decisions—conscious and subconscious—that have been made by its leaders and people over a long period of time.

A parish either refuses to see the damage being done by its stubborn inability to resolve internecine feuds, or it closes its eyes to the changing nature of the environment in which its property is situated, or it falls prey to a dozen other maladies that can afflict local congregations. Whatever the pathology, at this very moment many parishes around the United States are charting courses that will guarantee their extinction within a couple of generations, at the most. Yet a vast majority of them are in places where there is enormous potential to remain fertile Christian communities, even spawning daughter congregations! This frightening statistic should give us cause for thought: researchers believe that if present trends continue, sixty percent of all existing Christian congregations in America will disappear before the year 2050.[11] While the average American is a thirtysomething, the average Christian in a traditional denomination like our own is well over fifty. Given the demographics of the Episcopal Church, we are set to lose half of our present parishes within the next thirty years if we do not make some radical changes.

Having said this, however, not all church closures are bad. Some die for good reasons, such as massive population shifts, both rural and urban. Others consign themselves to extinction because they refuse to remove the scales from their eyes and are so blinded to the realities of their situation they are prevented from being a

---

11. Norman Shawchuck and Gustave Rath, *Benchmarks of Quality in the Church* (Nashville: Abingdon, 1994), p. 12.

church able to care for others and proclaim the Good News. Healthy congregations that will survive into the middle of the next century are those which encourage a strong spiritual life, make a fundamental commitment to formation for mission and ministry, strive after a high quality of community life, and are unapologetically evangelistic.

George Hunter notes in his study of healthy and "apostolic" congregations that while each congregation is different, there are four common threads:

- They have gone overboard on their study and living out of the Scriptures.
- They have gone overboard on the experience, teaching, and life of prayer.
- They have gone overboard on concern for those who are beyond the fold of the church.
- They have gone overboard on the Great Commission, and both at home and overseas they are committed to making Christ known.

Hunter continues:

A traditional congregation's main business, by contrast, is to nurture and care for its members and their children. Most traditional congregations [merely] hope for growth....However, the apostolic congregation's main business is outreach to pre-Christian people. That mission takes priority over ministry to the members. The outreach priority enables them to avoid what Roman Catholic missiologists call the "choke law" in which, after some growth, the church redirects the time and energy once devoted to outreach to care for its own members instead, which "chokes" the ongoing mission to the remaining undiscipled population.[12]

Most Episcopal congregations fit this description to a tee.

---

12. George G. Hunter III, *Church for the Unchurched* (Nashville: Abingdon, 1996), pp. 31-32.

The survival mentality that has dogged the Episcopal Church for so long has no place in the emerging world—Christ commissioned us not merely to exist, but to flourish! Church history is strewn with the wreckage of not merely parishes but whole Christian traditions that have "choked." This is a sobering reminder that there is no such thing as congregational or denominational permanence. Each must be born anew, with each rising generation, and that is the challenge now confronting us in the Episcopal Church.

SUMMARY

- Despite its importance being acknowledged by Christian leaders of all backgrounds, Episcopalians still suffer from evangelism phobia.

- Evangelism is the passport to healthy congregational life both now and in the future.

- Americans are not unresponsive to the gospel, but they are less likely than ever before to come to the church seeking answers to spiritual problems.

- New congregations are the best way to draw unreached people into Christian fellowship.

- Evangelistic ventures, especially new church-plants, are less risky if the proper information is applied to the process.

- We need to develop creativity, imagination, and a willingness to learn from Christians of other traditions.

- On present trends, sixty percent of all American congregations will disappear before 2050, probably a larger proportion of Episcopal parishes.

QUESTIONS FOR DISCUSSION

- Think, pray, then compile a list of the various different aspects of evangelism that make you uncomfortable.

- What do you think your parish can learn from other local congregations that have shown substantial growth over the last ten years? Identify the characteristics of congregational life and strategy that make for evangelism.

- Do you see your congregation making decisions that lead to death or do you see it planning for new life? If the former is true for you, what can you do to alter this situation?

- Which has the highest priority in your parish, mission to the unchurched and unreached, or ministry to existing members? Analyze the reason for your answer.

- Study Matthew 28:16-19 and Acts 1:1-9. What do Jesus' final words say to you as an individual and to your parish?

7

Beyond Survival

Do you remember James Carvell? You probably do; the flamboyant Louisianan who was the strategist behind President Clinton's 1992 election victory is not easy to forget. Throughout the campaign, Carvell had over his desk a sheet of paper on which was printed the words, "It's the economy, stupid!" Every time the campaign veered off course and started to dissipate, he would look at those words and try to stay focused.

For numerous congregations in the Episcopal Church today, their own parish economy is very much on their minds. This means that when flights of fancy wing upward from the visionaries in their midst, they are quickly drawn back to reality by the worried number-crunchers who say, in effect, "We can't do that—it's the money, stupid!" The truth is that more of our congregations than we would like to admit are in straightened financial circumstances.

Here are some of the raw financial facts that we need to digest; they will provide a strong dose of "reality therapy." Twenty years into the future, it seems very likely that few parishes with a membership of less than two hundred fifty will be economically viable *if* we insist on hanging onto our present models for ministry. These include the expectation that every congregation, whatever its size, *has* to have a full-time, seminary-trained priest. Add to this the problem of deferred maintenance and the cost of the care and upkeep of aging buildings, and more and more of a congregation's assets are going to be gobbled up. Quite simply, it is money—or, more precisely, the lack of it—that will determine future congregational lifestyles.

Even now there are ominous signs of this change, as Loren Mead reports. Between 1982 and 1992 the Diocese of Ohio, for example, went from seven congregations being served by part-time clergy to thirty-three, or thirty percent of all its parishes. These churches either have bi-vocational priests or are served by part-time clergy or ministry clusters. This change in the number of parishes that can afford full-time clergy leadership is replicated in any number of dioceses who can no longer keep up the traditional model. In more and more churches, the struggle to pay the priest's salary and to find the money for the increasing cost of keeping up buildings and diocesan assessments leaves no financial resources for evangelism, formation, parish programming, outreach, or any other facet of healthy congregational life. Loren Mead illustrates the close ties between costs and budgets by quoting a Presbyterian acquaintance: "Our experience in 1991 was that national mission giving declined exactly in proportion to the increase of medical insurance payments for the clergy."[1]

For far too many of us, preserving the status quo has become the dominant passion: survival at any cost. We have a fixation on maintaining "the church," but any notion of the apostolic mission to which Christ has called us is buried alive. A cry that almost every bishop increasingly hears when visiting parishes is, "Bishop, we'd be okay if we could just find four or five more families!" This is what the survival mentality sounds like when it echoes through a congregation's life, loud and clear.

Dwindling resources are not only a parish dilemma, however, because the same scenario is beginning to play itself out among the smaller, unendowed dioceses of the Episcopal Church. In some cases, it would take no more than a modest crisis to drive

---

1. Loren Mead, *Transforming Congregations for the Future* (Washington D.C.: The Alban Institute, 1994), p. 14.

the diocese into liquidation or force upon it other unpalatable options. Already one small diocese has found itself looking such a disaster in the face: as a result of a lawsuit with a schismatic congregation, which was thankfully resolved out of court, the Diocese of Quincy experienced several worrisome years. Now committed to a church-planting program, it looks as if it could draw back from the edge, but not all dioceses will be so fortunate.

Episcopalians are not alone as they struggle with such forces, for judicatories of most other mainline denominations are facing the same hard choices, with many of their equivalents to our dioceses close to insolvency. So, once again the dynamic is money. The call of God is being submerged beneath the will to survive. Staying alive has become more important than serving God.

Concerned about the health of local congregations, and aware of the damage done to the mission of the church when funds are constantly diverted to pay judicatory overheads, the three Episcopal dioceses in the state of Wisconsin have begun to explore some creative alternatives. One possibility is that while maintaining their distinct areas of oversight, the three dioceses will merge many of their bureaucratic and program functions. If something like this happens it will at least ease assessment pressures on parishes for a while and give them a little breathing space to rethink the way they approach their ministry.

Whether we are talking congregations or dioceses, however, if some radical changes are not made soon, as we enter the new millennium many more Christian parishes are going to be forced in some uncomfortable directions. To date the churches have done little to address this. So far we have cut budgets and applied band-aids, but it is obvious that such first aid does not work; the slide goes on. Loren Mead talks about the churches being tossed about in "a storm of considerable proportions," as we make our way through a landscape dotted with unexploded bombs![2] Only a radically different approach will suffice if we are to move beyond the present impasse.

---

2. Mead, _Transforming Congregations,_ p. 12.

∞ The Priority Must Be Mission

We have created an institutional structure which has the capacity to absorb vast quantities of time and energy just keeping it fed and watered—much to the detriment of the church's mission. When assessing the mission failures of the early church, the late South African missiologist David J. Bosch noted that the early church quickly

> ceased to be a movement and turned into an institution. There are essential differences between an institution and a movement:...the one is conservative, the other progressive; the one is more or less passive, yielding to influences from outside, the other is active, influencing rather than being influenced; the one looks to the past, the other to the future....In addition, we might add, the one is anxious, the other is prepared to take risks; the one guards boundaries, the other crosses them....As time went by, intra-ecclesial issues and the struggle for survival as a separate religious group consumed more and more of the energy of Christians.[3]

One reason for this struggle for survival, as we have seen already, is that yesterday's patterns of church life do not fit comfortably in today's strained and straining world. In a more stable and less chaotic era, when the hierarchical patterns of organization with which we have lived for so long functioned more smoothly, leaders found it possible to manage. They could coordinate and even control what already existed—as well as occasionally break new ground. The job of leaders, primarily the ordained but some lay persons too, was to "run the church" in an orderly way, providing religious services to those who deemed them necessary, which appeared to be a significant proportion of the population. In many respects, it was chaplaincy writ large.

Those expectations are no more. Today the church is no longer necessarily the first place to which people turn when looking for

---

3. David J. Bosch, *Transforming Mission* (Maryknoll, NY: Orbis Books, 1991), pp. 50-51.

spiritual succor, and except in a handful of suburban communities the "family-style church" that people half-remember from childhood and young adulthood is gone forever. Brand loyalty to a particular denominational tradition is also a thing of the past. If people do turn to the Christian community, it is less and less likely to be Episcopal or other old-line congregations that will draw them, with their graying membership and passion for archaic music and ancient language.

With an Episcopal median age of fiftysomething, large numbers of our parishes are made up predominantly of middle-aged and elderly people, and, quite naturally, the lives of these fellowships are as a result focused around the interests of this particular set of members. Add to that more than a quarter-century of short-sighted clergy recruitment policies, and we discover that today we have next to no young priests with whom Generation X might identify.

Yet it is the teenagers and twentysomethings who are traditionally the most open to the claims of the Christian faith, and are the ones in the largest numbers doing the spiritual searching. While the rootedness of our tradition attracts a significant proportion of these young people, they are hardly likely to feel very much at home in a religious community whose interests and ages are close to those of their parents or grandparents.

∞ Old Patterns of Ministry
One of the saddest experiences is to sit listening to a faithful, older priest attempting to put a positive spin on the depressing procession of parish statistics that have followed him[4] through most of his ministry. What do you say to encourage someone reaching the end of an active ministry, who has seen churches dwindle from full to almost empty? Without doubt such congregations have provided caring ministry over the years, but it does terrible things to the soul to watch a parish shrink so rapidly that more children

---

4. Women were not ordained to the priesthood until well into the numerical decline which has pressed in upon the Episcopal Church.

were in Sunday school thirty years ago than the total attendance on Easter Sunday now.

The old patterns of pastoral ministry in which such clergy were schooled were obviously deficient when it came to proclaiming the gospel. In his book *The Impossible Vocation*, John Snow tells his own story from the 1950s as he diagnoses the problems of many clergy, both then and now. Among other things, Snow points out that most seminarians of his vintage were schooled in an inadequate understanding of the doctrine of salvation. When the doctrine of salvation was trivialized, it followed that justification by faith through grace was difficult both to understand and to assimilate. Consequently, seminarians were never formed in a realistic and theological understanding of the depths of human sin. "Seminary exposure to theology then," Snow writes, "was for many of us superficial; to a degree it was even spiritually damaging. We acquired an overlay of theological material which we could recite on demand, seizing bits and pieces of theology eclectically, here and there, which fit into our customarily empirical and psychotherapeutic way of thinking."[5]

Little has changed. This therapeutic approach to belief survives and flourishes to this day, and has become almost inextricably integrated into our traditional perception that congregations be modeled after old-fashioned village churches. In this scenario, the "parson" also becomes the chaplain and therapist. We have as a result created an organization that at times seems almost incapable of speaking to the spiritual condition of increasing numbers of today's people. In addition, those who have shaped the agenda of the church at the national level for the last several generations have tended to be more "liberal" than the bulk of a population who, if they are seeking after truth at all, are looking for an expression of faith that is theologically more "conservative."[6]

---

5. John Snow, *The Impossible Vocation* (Cambridge, MA: Cowley Publications, 1988), pp. 10-11.

6. Lyle Schaller, *It's a Different World!* (Nashville: Abingdon, 1987), p. 76.

∞ *It's a Different World!*

At the parish level, the church has continued to function as if it believed that the majority population will continue to be of European extraction, will speak English as its first language, and will, for reasons of ancestry, be drawn to Christianity. Yet today's world of increasing pluralism does not work in the same way our more monochrome past did. America is increasingly multi-ethnic. Larger numbers of people do not speak English at home, and many, especially Asians, do not come from backgrounds that are either historically Christian or even monotheistic. Furthermore, most first-generation immigrants do not cast off the cultures with which they grew up; that remains for their children and grand-children to do.

Although Spanish-speaking Episcopalians have done a credit-able job reaching out to the growing Hispanic population in the United States, only a handful of North American Anglicans have sought to reach out to the other ethnic groups who are crowding in. Perhaps our failure to do so starkly illustrates the theological deficiency of which John Snow so eloquently speaks: if we do not understand the breathtaking implications of salvation and re-demption, sharing the gospel is unlikely to be a passion in our lives. Furthermore, increasing numbers of Christians, and perhaps a majority of the clergy, are hesitant to make the claim that there is anything qualitatively different between the Christian faith and other religions. This fact was starkly illustrated in a recent report that a parish priest in the Diocese of Pittsburgh gave of a visit from an aspiring missionary whose ministry was to focus on a group of people who are among the least evangelized in the world. When asked if he had tried to serve as an appointee of the national church, the missionary said that the executive with whom he interviewed there castigated him for even entertaining the idea that Buddhists need to know the message of Jesus Christ.[7]

In addition, a large proportion of Americans no longer live in the family units that once made it easy for the churches to serve

---

7. *The Living Church* (May 5, 1996).

them. Today's America has more single adults living alone than ever before, as well as blended families, couples who live together but are delaying marriage or do not consider it an option, and an explosion of single-parent households. Leonard Sweet writes:

> Almost three out of ten homes are single-parent families. Sixty-six percent of African American children are being born to single women, according to the latest figures. The population of singles in America is skyrocketing—in 1970 the percentage of the US population age 19 and older that were single was 32 percent women, 22 percent men; in 1990 it had climbed to 40 percent women, 36 percent men. From 1960 to 1990, the proportion of adults living alone tripled, from 4 to 12 percent of the population. The most recent census counts 22 million people living alone, over one in four households.[8]

Add to this a whole throng of identity issues, like those related to gender and sexuality, and modern society is an extremely complex phenomenon with which yesterday's patterns of ministry are never going to cope.

Congregations that have sought to reach into these growing "non-traditional" networks have found the work harder and financially more draining than anything they have ever attempted. Creativity and perseverance are needed, and very often we are short on both. Perhaps one of the most unreached mission fields in the United States today is the one on our doorsteps: the vast complexes of apartments that are mushrooming around the beltways of our cities, many almost completely oblivious to the Christian message. The vast majority of units in these developments are leased by single men and women, many of whose apparent self-absorption is little more than a thin veneer covering an aching emptiness.

In addition, a radical change in employment patterns has stripped congregations of much of the built-in volunteer force they once depended on: married women who do not work outside

---

8. Leonard Sweet, *FaithQuakes* (Nashville: Abingdon, 1994), p. 31.

the home. As late as a generation ago, a significant proportion of such women remained out of the paid workforce at least while their children were very small. Today, either because of their career commitments or because of pressing financial needs, after marriage and while still childbearing, the vast majority of women are stretched to the limit juggling family and employment. Furthermore, married women are some of the finest small business entrepreneurs in America today, and many a "kitchen table" operation has become a healthy profitable business under their wise leadership. The church loses invaluable resources when such women's talents are lost to the church as their time and energy for volunteerism declines.

∞ Scanning the Horizon

Parishes held hostage by the survival mentality seem unable to break out of yesterday's mold, and are still determined to try and make an approach to ministry which is doomed work. It is little wonder that Christians in such congregations get frustrated and burn out when they discover how few dividends this mode of operation pays today. The gospel imperative is to proclaim Christ in word and deed. If we are to do this effectively in a fast-altering environment, this could well mean jettisoning attitudes and patterns that hold us back, while trying to identify from our tradition those things which might be helpful. Leonard Sweet suggests that faithful churches in the future will be those who manage to be "AncientFuture": that is, they are congregations grounded in a rich, biblical tradition, but their eyes will be constantly scanning the distant horizon.

Rather than tinkering with present structures and institutions—like trying to prolong the life of an old car—we should be carefully looking at the realities, and then in a visionary manner allowing the creative juices of all the people of God to flow freely. The impetus for this forward movement usually has to come from the priest, who should be self-assured enough not to be threatened when the laypeople take hold and bring the transforming message of Jesus Christ out from the church into all the world. Yesterday's contact points with the unchurched population may have dried up, but there are a thousand and one new ones emerging. Our job is to find and to nourish them.

For example, how many parishes have tried to reach out to people by presenting workshops for children hurt by the divorce of their parents, or to be a place where adults who are struggling with their chaotic finances can get loving help and assistance in unraveling their tangled web of affairs and learn to live within a budget? Some churches try ideas like these but often do little to follow through on the contacts made; they offer a "social service" but in no way invite people to meet the living Christ. We are convinced that in this spiritually hungry age parishes could present imaginative courses in twenty-first century spirituality; such courses would help them make contact with those who are on a journey but who might flounder into vacuous New Age spirituality unless Christ is shown to be relevant to their struggles today.

It is vital that our congregations work out how to minister to Generation X and their children. This may mean learning how to make forays into the cyber-communities fast developing all over the Internet and exploring ways of presenting the gospel online. As Leonard Sweet writes:

> New forms of human community and "being" community are already coming out of communications technology. If the church does not reflexively condemn these new forms of family life, the church can help shape them morally and ensure that families will be rich and authentic and uplifting of the human spirit.[9]

Some of the finest innovators on the Internet are not Christian but neopagan groups who have used computers to follow the occult practice of "casting a circle," for example.[10] Christians must learn how to enter this new world of cyberspace as well.

---

9. Sweet, *FaithQuakes*, p. 31.
10. Culled from the June 1996 issue of *Religion Watch*, a newsletter which monitors trends in contemporary religion.

∽ Turning Liabilities into Assets

It would help a great deal if we could to get beyond seeing our heritage—particularly our architectural heritage—as a problem. Many congregations are weighed down by the cost of maintaining a property that is used for only a few hours every week. Any business that employed its real estate as ineffectively as churches would have filed for bankruptcy protection years ago! Again, creative thinking is necessary. Congregations and clergy need to ask the right questions about how to transform buildings that are a drain on resources into an asset for a missionary people.

Here is one possibility. In an age of downsizing, when more and more people are being forced into business on their own, and where small, homegrown businesses are beginning to flourish, there are all sorts of people looking for affordable office space. Those offices need to be accessible to the renter's home, to the business community, to schools where children are being educated, and they need to be easy to locate for people visiting them. With its array of classrooms which stand empty from Sunday to Sunday, what is there to prevent a congregation from transforming some or all its excess space into such offices?

Not only would this force churches to upgrade their drab, often unplastered concrete block facilities and put some decent carpeting on the floors, it would also provide a service to entrepreneurs and nonprofit start-up businesses. A lockable, built-in office could be installed in each room, and leases could be worked out that enabled the businessperson to share the room with the parish. The parish secretary could be receptionist for these folks, and they could even have access to the copier and fax machine. The parlor or parish lounge could be a place which they could borrow for larger meetings when the church did not need it, and the church coffee pot, would, in effect, become the water cooler and meeting place.

Such a strategy would accomplish several things at once. It would provide a service to young businesses, enabling those who are starting from scratch to work with colleagues in neighboring offices, thus breaking the cycle of loneliness that tends to afflict those who work on their own. It would force a church to upgrade its facilities, making them far more attractive to a young couple, say, who are looking for a church home but who are put off by the church-basement style of architecture that may have satisfied their grandparents in the years following World War II. After the cost of improvements have been paid for, the rents paid by the businesses would assist with the overhead of maintaining the building and the church office. The changes would make the parish plant look less of a forbidding "religious hulk" and much more of a community center. In such a setting a congregation could showcase its ministry to those who work there, or visitors who come to do business with them.

Welcoming new businesses into the building is a wonderful way to make unchurched people familiar with the insides of a church building and break the "threshold shock" most people experience if they have little experience of a believing community. It is also an opportunity for the clergy, most of whom tend to get very bound up in church life, to rub shoulders with—and even live out Christ to—those whose whole lifestyle has never before brought them into contact with the church.

By applying a measure of creativity to ministry, there is much that can be done to neutralize the deadening effects of the church's "survival mentality." These are only a few ideas to get people started, and we are convinced there are manifold opportunities staring our congregations in the face—if they were but to see them. At its heart this process is theological, with profound practical implications for everything from the episcopate to the humblest rural mission. To be a going concern in the new century, we need to start thinking in these ways now.

∽ What About the Clergy?

We have noted already that the seminaries and clergy selection processes require radical reengineering if they are to train the different kind of clergy who are capable of exercising ministry in the future. In addition, every resource we can muster has to be focused on equipping "all the saints" for the work of ministry.

Right now the church is trapped by its own inflexibility, but a great fermentation is taking place in our midst and old wineskins can no longer contain it. Our preoccupation with maintenance is tantamount to a death wish, inhibiting the forward movement of the gospel.

If local congregations, both large and small, are to be reinvigorated for mission, three areas need to be addressed. The first is *episcope*, or the ministry of the bishop. In light of everything we have said, it is essential that our understanding of the bishop's job be revised along with the job description itself. In addition, we need to reassess the function of priests and deacons. Meanwhile, we should be working out how this will reshape the ministry of all the baptized.

Bishops are in a predicament. The expectations now laid upon them are inappropriate and overwhelming. Theological and existential realities are almost constantly in tension with each other. Work has begun in various forums to address this issue, but it needs to be given higher priority. It is essential that we shift our understanding of the bishop's role from that of CEO of a "religious bus" to that of chief evangelist, teacher, and pastor. There is much we can learn from episcopal patterns in other areas of the Anglican Communion.

Perhaps one of the most exciting dioceses in the Anglican world today is the Diocese of Nelson in New Zealand. Their bishop, Derek Eaton, after service in the Middle East with the Church Missionary Society of New Zealand, returned to ministry at home and took on a small struggling seaside parish. In four years the congregation grew sixfold, and as a result, Derek was elected bishop! In his first five years as Bishop of Nelson, which is on New Zealand's South Island, the diocese grew by one-third—and this in a country which many consider the most secular in the world. Bishop Eaton, writing recently about his ministry, commented:

> A bishop is principally called to be a missionary, teacher, and evangelist, not an administrator. [Alice and I] are in parishes

nearly every weekend as well as in the week. We stay with the clergy, sitting around the kitchen, encouraging, praying, and discussing. They see a lot of us. I see myself as a talent scout recognizing people's gifts and releasing them in ministry. Leaders need to appoint to their weaknesses. I have a highly motivated team around me with gifts I don't have....We encourage our clergy to do good expository biblical teaching. If you raise the spiritual temperature, other things tend to fall into place.[11]

By leading from the front, Bishop Eaton has made mission a priority in his diocese, and the results are there for all to see. It is clear that when mission becomes the overarching priority of the diocese, a congregation, or a local network of parishes, substantial structural change is bound to take place. This in turn reallocates the way in which the church uses its precious resources, as well as the manner in which it deploys its personnel. All this means that not only is the job of the bishop going to be different in the future, the clergy will also be used in a variety of different ways, necessitating the intentional recruitment of personnel with appropriate potential to be trained to work with the exciting uncertainty of emerging models.

As far as the deployment of priests and deacons goes, changing patterns raise enormous issues that need immediate attention. If we refuse to take up the challenges and merely sustain present ministry patterns, cycles of decline and blame will keep us spiraling downward. For example, serious consideration needs to be given to training and utilizing "local priests" in more imaginative ways than our present Canon IX allows. We suspect that more and more clergy will be asked to be pioneers, which means that they will probably have to find additional employment to help fund their ministry. We must continue to reevaluate what dia-

---

11. Derek Eaton's article "From Maintenance to Mission" was first published in *Reach Out,* the bulletin of the Episcopal Church Missionary Community, then reprinted in *The Anglican Digest* (Pentecost 1996).

conal service means, and how the ministry of deacons supports and clarifies the ministries of priests and lay people. Then we can ask what the eucharistic community really is, and whether lay celebration of the eucharist is appropriate to missionary situations, while seriously keeping in mind the need for order in the church.

All of the above is dependent upon the recognition that mission is the work of all the baptized, and therefore it is essential that every resource possible, human and financial, be focused on enabling the laity in their ministry. Until now, the tendency has been to "allow" the laity to pick up the odds and ends of ministry that the ordained do not want; in tomorrow's world, we court disaster if we continue this pattern rather than enabling lay men and women to be full participants in the whole ministry of the church—for which the Holy Spirit has already equipped them. Permission-giving churches with a passion for mission are "discovering the foolishness of committee work, and the importance of spiritual gifts.... When people discover how God created them to function within the Body, the church comes alive with ministry to people rather than going to endless rounds of meetings."[12]

If congregations prayerfully are seeking God's will, they will be aware of the deep need there is for change, and will start implementing some very different policies. If this happens, then ours will be a very different church by 2015. Now is the time to explore a variety of approaches which break the old mold. It is vital that a new breed of spiritually alert risk-takers comes to the fore supported by national, diocesan, and local resources. Alongside the radical restructuring necessary at a national level, the time is here to identify and slaughter a whole procession of diocesan and parochial sacred cows. This is not change for change's sake, but because old ways of doing things that are symptomatic of the survival mentality stand in the way of Christ's mission and the advance of God's Kingdom.

---

12. William Easum, *Sacred Cows Make Gourmet Burgers* (Nashville: Abingdon, 1995), pp. 62-63.

As you look to the future, consider these tough questions. By the year 2020, many of our generation will have "gone to glory"! What does your congregation have to offer Generation X and their children as they crowd our nurseries and schools during their formative first ten years? Have you sought to understand their spiritual needs and where they are coming from? If you fail to address these questions, your congregation, as part of one of America's aging, old-line denominations, will have condemned itself to fading into the sunset because it has missed the point and has been struggling to maintain an untenable status quo.

When we started writing the article—that would eventually turn into this chapter—about the challenges facing congregations with less than two hundred fifty members, we did not realize the depth and extent of the problem. We quickly realized that more often than not such parishes are dollar-driven. If we continue to walk this path and allow money to dictate the agenda, all our worst fears will be realized. However, if we are prepared to take calculated risks and make some of the necessary radical changes, a new day could very well be dawning. It's not the money, it's the mission!

SUMMARY

- In many parishes and ministries, vision is squashed by cautious number-crunching and the survival mentality.

- By 2015 most of the parishes with less than two hundred fifty members will not be able to function as they do today, if they are in existence at all.

- The same dilemma facing congregations faces dioceses and the national church.

- These emerging challenges demand a total, and creative, commitment to evangelism and mission.

- We ignore the needs of Generation X and their children at our peril.

- The village parish model, with its overlay of therapeutic theory, both of which have shaped our ministry in the past, no longer cuts the ice.

- The world has changed, as has the way we make contact with outsiders, but few congregations have gone out to meet these challenges.

- Apparent liabilities—such as aging and underused church buildings—can be turned into assets.

- The way clergy minister in the church has to be radically rethought.

QUESTIONS FOR DISCUSSION

- How much is your congregation's mission shaped and determined by money?

- What role do you think funds, or the lack of them, should play in structuring the mission of the church?

- What thought have you given to reaching Generation X and their children?

- If you could no longer afford a full-time priest, how would it change the shape of your congregation's ministry?

- Study 1 Corinthians 12-14 and Ephesians 4:1-16. What do you think Paul is saying about the future shape of ministry?

- Do you have underutilized space in your parish plant? What ideas do you have about turning these liabilities into assets?

- Spend some time visioning how bishops could be bishops in different ways. How could we use the service of "local priests"? What needs to be put in place to enhance the ministry of the laity and to identify their gifts?

8

Radically Rethinking Global Mission

S ay the word "church" in most small study or focus groups, and what occurs to a majority of people are images that reveal a strikingly thin understanding of the breadth of the church. We use the word "church" to describe everything from the building in which a congregation meets to the denominational body to which a particular congregation happens to belong. Few of us have more than a fleeting grasp of the church's global dimension. Yet the Episcopal Church belongs to a worldwide communion that is part of a major stream of Christian commitment in God's one holy catholic and apostolic church, or, as the 1662 *Book of Common Prayer* put it, the church "militant here in earth."

This global dimension has been sorely underemphasized in much Episcopal thinking and in many parishes for a large proportion of the last two generations, as reflected in how we have established and pursued our priorities and in our tendency to look inward rather than outward. The reasons for our global timidity are complex, but among them is the nagging doubt of some, and the outright denial by others, that the Christian message is universally applicable. Whereas earlier generations were confident that Jesus Christ is "the way, the truth, and the life," as written in the Gospel of John, since World War II increasing numbers have not been so sure.

A further element in our global retreat has been a growing tendency to think locally and act locally. The only time we think in wider terms is while passing resolutions about political conflicts or macro-economic issues at our conventions, of which few, if any, will take any notice. Jesus sent his disciples into "all the world," but for too many of us mission dribbles into insignificance the further we get from our own hometown. It is a sad fact that the Episcopal Church's global engagement is minimal when compared to other denominations.

We have all heard the arguments offered by good and worthy Christians who, when we talk of the world reach of our faith, adamantly insist there is so much to be done here that it is almost irresponsible to send resources overseas. This insularity is often illustrated by the comments of and decisions made by local parish leaders who insist that their priority must be to take care of the parish first—which usually means preserving the church building or providing a comfortable salary for a priest.

Loren Mead's fine analysis of the end of the "Christendom paradigm" in *The Once and Future Church* is deeply moving, but in his enthusiasm to press home a point that needs constant repetition—that in a secularized America, the mission field has returned to our own doorsteps—he temporarily loses sight of the gospel's global panorama. This perception then plays into the justifiable queasiness of Episcopalians who have come to harbor guilt about past colonialism under the auspices of religion. For them this attitude transforms involvement in world mission from what could be the joyful task of bringing light to the world into an act of cultural imperialism.

While difficult questions about past missionary activities need to be addressed, this perception seems to reflect not only an anachronistic understanding of global mission, but a lack of familiarity with what actually is happening in mission around the world. Episcopalians played a significant role in the great missionary movement of the past two hundred years; it certainly had its flaws, but the time has come to take a good look at the global church—and to get the facts straight.[1] The old days of missionaries in pith helmets are long gone, and today's evangelists work as servants of the servants of God in burgeoning Two-Thirds World churches. They are more likely to be sitting at a computer in a city office and straining to keep up with immigration from the countryside, or networking the provision of resources from one part of the global church to another, or helping to produce intelligent and culturally pertinent Christian resources and publications, than they are to be bouncing through the bush in a four-wheel drive vehicle.

Anyone who attended the Global Conference for Dynamic Evangelism Beyond the Year 2000 (or G-CODE 2000) in Kanuga, North Carolina, in September 1995 departed with no doubt that millions around the world are beneficiaries of the vision of our forebears, and that the Episcopal Church is part of a dynamic global family of churches, the worldwide Anglican Communion. This conference was, in effect, the mid-Decade of Evangelism evaluation of the Anglican Communion's mission and evangelistic progress. Representatives gathered in Kanuga from fifty-four different countries for what many present considered one of the most exciting events they ever attended.

Furthermore, any lingering illusions that we westerners are the leaders of this family of churches were quickly dispelled at the conference. The center of gravity of worldwide Anglicanism has moved away from the North Atlantic to the global South; the Episcopal Church is but a modest part of this dynamic communion. Such incredible progress is being made elsewhere that each day we grow proportionately smaller when compared to African or Asian churches. So it is vital that when we speak of "the church"

---

1. Richard Kew and Cyril Okorocha's book, *Vision Bearers* (Harrisburg, PA: Morehouse Publishing, 1996), is an attempt to provide an overview of the Anglican Communion and the exciting story of its missionary engagement as it prepares for the twenty-first century.

we hold at the front of our minds its global dimensions. There is a tremendous educational task ahead of us as we share the story and point out tomorrow's possibilities. It is essential for the health of even the tiniest local congregation that it discover how it can play its part on the world scene.

∽ A Radically Changing World

The paradigm of Christendom is passing in the West at the very moment global culture is giving birth to a whole new civilization. Past chapter changes, like the Renaissance and Reformation, have usually had a modest beginning in one particular geographical area. Then slowly, like the ripples of a pond, the impact spreads outward. Industrialization, which began transforming the West two-hundred and fifty years ago, is still spreading into remote corners of the planet. Meanwhile, the information culture that is coming into being is overtaking it in other places.

In 1980 Alvin Toffler argued in *The Third Wave* that if the first wave of human civilization was the agricultural revolution and the second was the industrial revolution, the information revolution is ushering in the third wave of human culture. Quantum culture began in a whole variety of different spots, and is affecting many places all at once, sped along by instant electronic communication and relative ease of travel. Like a fast-moving torrent it jostles the foundations of every institution that gets in its way—from multinational corporations to the way we organize our families and our local congregations. It brings with it turmoil, turning us into "the last generation of an old civilization and the first generation of a new one."[2] Observers and experts gather in many settings on every continent to discuss the implications of what is happening, for it is challenging everything from world commerce to the viability of the nation state.

"We are speeding," the Tofflers write, "toward a different structure of power that will create...a world...sharply divided

---

2. Alvin and Heidi Toffler, *Creating a New Civilization* (Atlanta: Turner Publishing, 1995), p. 21.

into three contrasting and competing civilizations—the first still symbolized by the hoe, the second by the assembly line, and the third by the computer." While those at the bottom of the international pecking order continue to scratch a precarious living from the unforgiving soil, they continue,

> Third Wave nations [have started to] sell information and innovation, management, culture and pop culture, advanced technology, software, education, training, medical care and financial and other services to the world. One of those services might well also turn out to be military protection based on its command of superior Third Wave forces.[3]

While this different and unpredictable world is being born, we find ourselves interconnected as never before. We had just become accustomed to using direct dialing around the world when the fax machine appeared, and together these accelerated the metabolism of communication. Then the Internet burst in upon us. When the nineties began, e-mail was an arcane pursuit of a few academics and a handful of forward-looking corporations. Now people who used to get anxious about making long-distance phone calls rush home from work in the evening to talk to strangers all over the world through their online service.

Recently one of us stopped in at a lunch place in the middle of Tennessee. Catching the English accent, the server started talking about her soon-to-be fiancé, who also happened to be English. She had "met" him online late one night when she was surfing the Internet. Until she had gone to Britain to visit him, she had hardly ever been out of the South, and yet now she was preparing to marry him, and they were trying to work out in which country they would live! If new modes of communication can alter individual and family lives so radically, there is no telling about their long-term impact on the world—or the potential they offer the church as it exercises its global ministry.

---

3. Toffler, _Creating a New Civilization_, p. 31.

Yet there is a dark underbelly to this revolution that is taking place. Communications technologies not only provide new opportunities to build creative relationships, they also blur the boundaries we used to draw between the local, the national, and the international. In some places, far from bringing unity, modern communications have been used most effectively to assert differences, deepen hatreds, and magnify animosities. In today's world the whole concept of the nation-state might be in danger because people feel so interconnected that they want to assert their ethnic, religious, or national identity, rather than being lost in one huge "generic" country, continent, or world. Within countries smaller ethnic groups want ever more independence: Siberia wants freedom from Moscow, Southern Sudan from the Arab north, and Scotland from England. In other places ancient tribal animosities are brought into play. Robert D. Kaplan, in his study entitled *The Ends of the Earth,* notes that countries such as Somalia and Liberia have now been carved up into domains presided over by competing warlords, while government in other "ethnoregions" is turning into "whatever can be managed at the local level."

Kaplan presents a bleak vision of the future, wondering whether the map of the future will be

> an ever-mutating representation of cartographic chaos: in some areas benign, or even productive, and in some areas violent. Because this map will always be changing, it may be updated, like weather reports, and transmitted daily over the Internet in those places that have reliable electricity or private generators. On this map, the rules by which diplomats and other policymaking elites have ordered the world these past few hundred years will apply less and less. Solutions, in the main, will have to come from within the affected cultures themselves.[4]

---

4. Robert D. Kaplan, *The Ends of the Earth: A Journey at the Dawn of the 21st Century* (New York: Random House, 1996), p. 335.

Other observers suggest that our interconnectedness presages an unprecedented "clash of civilizations," even religious wars, especially in those regions where major cultures, like tectonic plates, meet, overlap, and rub up against one another. The last few years are replete with evidence of this, the former Adriatic nation of Yugoslavia being a prime example.

In addition, events and catastrophes in once-remote places now have a way of spilling over into the rest of the world and affecting all of us. Global problems which may seem distant now are bound to profoundly influence our future. Millions of people live one meal away from starvation, and are unlikely to have access to potable water or, in the world's biggest cities, even breathable air. Disease is rampant. Burgeoning birth rates amidst appalling squalor are putting such stress upon the environment that some countries are already living on borrowed time, and these desperate conditions bring into being marauding armies of the dispossessed. Tribal and religious wars are simmered in such pots, the ever-expanding mega-cities are bringing them to the boil, and terrorists have the means to transport the resultant anger everywhere.

A realist cannot be sanguine about some of the challenges facing us in the coming century. Samuel P. Huntingdon, a respected professor at Harvard, foresees a possible "rest against the West" scenario.[5] This chilling prospect is understandable when we realize that just as communications enable us to see more clearly the plight of the downtrodden, those in less affluent parts of the world are also able to watch us as we live out our lives in the world's wealthy quadrant. When they watch television and see the world in which they think we all live, millions are eager to come here and get their piece of the pie. We may not be far into the next century before we see unprecedented mass migrations of peoples—which we will be incapable of controlling—into

---

5. We recommend reading Samuel P. Huntingdon's article "The Clash of Civilizations?" in the Summer 1993 edition of *Foreign Affairs*, Paul Kennedy's *Preparing for the Twenty-First Century* (New York: Random House, 1993), and Kaplan's *The Ends of the Earth*.

the wealthy, information-rich world. As Paul Kennedy has predicted:

> If the developing world remains caught in its poverty trap, the
> more developed countries will come under siege from tens of
> millions of migrants and refugees eager to reside among the
> prosperous but aging populations of the democracies. [6]

To a small degree this migration has already begun. We are all
aware of the hundreds of millions of dollars being spent to
maintain the integrity of the border between the United States
and Mexico. One-third of all Russians visiting the United States
attempt to settle here as illegal immigrants, while shiploads of
Chinese immigrants are making their way here illegally.

∽ *A New Global Commitment*

It is into this world that we are sent to proclaim that salvation is
to be found in the risen Lord Jesus Christ. Clearly such a world
calls us not only to a new global commitment, but also challenges
us to put together the relationships and structures which will
enable us to share both our material and our spiritual bounty with
one another. While in the past theological liberals have, quite
rightly, castigated their more conservative sisters and brothers for
reducing evangelism to little more than talk, evangelicals are
equally right when they criticize those elsewhere on the theological spectrum for seeming to view the church as nothing more than
a deliverer of social services or a supporter of causes. Our message
is that in Christ the Kingdom of God is in our midst: proclamation, justice, grace, and truth are all part of one another in the
New Creation.

One of the most pressing challenges before Christians in the
years ahead will be to discover how we might live the gospel in
the midst of global turbulence, and how we make Christ known.
This will mean allowing Christians elsewhere in the world to shine
their critical spotlights on us and our churches; they have already

6. Kennedy, *Preparing for the Twenty-First Century*, p. 46.

started to ask how we can justify the lavishness of our lifestyle and vast consumption of the world's cheap labor and limited resources.

While the world has been turning into the global village Marshall McLuhan foresaw, the church around the world has matured. Those churches planted as a result of the often-criticized missionary activity of the western churches have become strong and confident; their perspective enables them to see the spiritual hollowness of the industrialized West. Given the strategic importance of the West in the global church, increasing numbers from these younger churches are eager to become involved with what Lesslie Newbigin calls "the most difficult missionary frontier in the contemporary world."[7]

It is conceivable that some of the new life that will pour into our churches by the year 2015 will be inspired and led by Christians from countries like Ghana, Uganda, Malaysia, or Chile who come to North America and western Europe as missionaries impelled by the power of the Holy Spirit.[8] We are on the verge of discovering, as did the early Christians, just how much global mission is a multidimensional activity. The time is at hand when Anglicans elsewhere in the world are putting the Episcopal Church under the microscope and finding it wanting, and yearn to share in its life so that they can make a difference.

∞ New Beginnings in the Episcopal Church

This brief international overview portrays the environment in which all the churches are increasingly being forced to minister. The changes taking place are both wrenching and revolutionary. Such a profound reconstruction of the world inevitably calls upon us to totally rethink, and then to rework, our global engagement—and the time is late for beginning such a process. Most of

---

7. Lesslie Newbigin, *Unfinished Agenda* (London: SPCK and Grand Rapids, MI: Eerdmans, 1985), p. 249.

8. For a discussion of this new missionary wave see Kew and Okorocha, *Vision Bearers*, p. 40.

yesterday's preconceptions need to be abandoned, either because their theology is inadequate, or because they no longer work.

The late David Bosch, one of the most creative theologians of mission of our time, concluded his final book with the words, "The mission of the church needs constantly to be renewed and reconceived." He pointed out that critics of mission have usually begun from the supposition that mission is western Christians going out to save souls and to impose their will upon others. We have seen already that whatever else may be true, the western churches are no longer in control of global mission—which, Bosch reminds us, begins at the cross, the place of humiliation and judgment. Yet, paradoxically, the cross is also "the place of refreshment and new birth." The church is "the community of the cross...the fellowship of the Kingdom," and its task is to invite people "to a feast without end." The church's mission must, again and again, be reshaped as it is subsumed into God's mission, the *misseo Dei.*[9]

It was perhaps inevitable that a decision made on financial grounds in an attempt to protect the budget of the national church should, providentially, turn out to be the stimulus which has led us to begin to ask fundamental questions about the nature and structure of our global engagement in the future. Early in 1994 the world mission program of the Episcopal Church was suddenly thrust into the limelight by a decision of the Executive Council to cut back—or even eliminate—the missionary engagement of the national church. Under budgetary pressure, the force of Appointed Missionaries and Volunteers for Mission was already shrinking; the plan was to phase it out altogether. The rationale behind this idea was that mission should become the work of a growing number of voluntary mission agencies, specialists in the equipping and sending of personnel. These agencies, it was argued, are able to focus upon this task far more effectively than an ecclesiastical bureaucracy. We believe that in principle this was

---

9. David Bosch, *Transforming Mission* (Maryknoll, NY: Orbis Books, 1991), p. 519.

the right direction in which to be moving, but good decisions and appropriate processes are seldom put in place when the real effort is to protect dwindling resources.

As soon as the decision was made public, a cry went up from both old and young. A father figure of foreign mission in the Episcopal Church, Charles Long, an old China hand, asked how the Episcopal Church could call itself the Domestic *and Foreign* Missionary Society if it were to abandon its global commitments in this way. To many people this decision seemed the most flagrant example of the Episcopal Church, like so much of American culture, becoming self-absorbed and isolationist. Our past deep commitment to world mission had already been relegated to the periphery; now the time had come to spin it off altogether. Saving money had come to take precedence over the mission to which the church is called of proclaiming Christ.

We think that this misjudgment may have begun with the Executive Council's "Listening Process" in 1993, when senior officials went out to the dioceses and congregations of the church in order to hear what people at the parish level held as important. Mission seemed to be a low priority with those at the grassroots, and the council heard little opinion expressed about it. While global ministry in the Episcopal Church has not had the attention it receives in other traditions for many years, we surmise that one reason little interest was shown in mission could have been that the wrong questions were asked.

In any case the fox was loose in the hen-house, and a great deal of feverish activity went on during the lead up to the 1994 General Convention in Indianapolis. We were both present at the New Wineskins missions conference at Ridgecrest, North Carolina, in April 1994, almost the first occasion in living memory when more than five hundred Episcopalians met to celebrate and learn about the challenge the world offers. Beneath the surface of that exciting gathering the Executive Council decision was the source of considerable anxiety. Seventeen resolutions from all over the country arrived in Indianapolis. When boiled down to six they resulted in the Convention restoring, and in some cases even increasing, much of the world mission funding as a major priority of the church's official program.

The 1994 actions of the Executive Council may turn out to have been a blessing, because one of those six resolutions also appealed for a total rethinking and "re-visioning" of the way we approach our global responsibilities. This debacle drew together a broad-based coalition of those engaged in world mission and those willing to make the point with passion that global action is vital to the church's future health and wholeness. A task force made up of members of the Standing Commission for World Mission (SCWM) and the Episcopal Council for Global Mission (ECGM) came into being within months of Indianapolis, and set about exploring the possibilities.

This task force provided a wonderful opportunity to dream afresh how we might address the global challenge in the new millennium. As the old world crumbles, so do the mission structures with which we reach into the world. Twenty years ago virtually every aspect of our global encounter was managed out of the Episcopal Church Center, but today only a portion of the church's global engagement is tied in with the Anglican and Global Affairs office in New York, and more local initiatives are being born all the time. In the last generation a cadre of specialized volunteer agencies have come into being and gained momentum, maturity, and increased stature in the church. For example, the South American Missionary Society (SAMS), founded in 1976, gave new impetus to the provision of personnel to the expanding churches of Latin America, and is today one of the fastest growing mission agencies in North America. The Episcopal Church Missionary Community (ECMC) has been encouraging various facets of education, prayer, and training for nearly a quarter of a century, while the Anglican Frontier Missions, established in 1992, is attempting to develop new formulas for taking the gospel to the world's least evangelized peoples.

Today a number of parishes and dioceses, both large and small, are sending out their own partners to work overseas, while large congregations like Truro Church and the Church of the Apostles, both in Fairfax, Virginia, have global mission commitments which outstrip those of most dioceses. Episcopalians also play a major part in ecumenical and interdenominational activities, and can be found doing everything from planting churches among the Khazak people to translating the Bible in remote corners of the globe. The renewing of the Episcopal Church's relationship with the Russian Orthodox Church has opened up countless possibilities for both individuals and parishes in Russia and Ukraine, while a steady stream of companion relationships between dioceses here and elsewhere in the Anglican Communion (and beyond) continues to grow.

Much goes on at the level of grassroots mission through this network of companion relationships and partnerships. These have often given Episcopalians a taste of new life in Christ as Anglican Christians from Chile to Uganda, and believers in Moscow and Shanghai, have been linked with groups of Episcopalians. It seems that many of the most productive global involvements today are those that begin at the grassroots, and it is a great pity that we make such limited use of these opportunities. Furthermore, while there has been a significant decline in full-time "career" missionaries, increasing numbers of Episcopalians are sharing their skills all over the world as they undertake short-term missions—very often at their own expense, or supported by those they have solicited. Programs like those organized by SOMA (Sharing of Ministry Abroad) have given hundreds of Episcopalians first-hand experience of the global church. Such programs illustrate that, if properly challenged, Episcopalians *will* get involved. In addition to the young people who have gone abroad on assignments with SOMA or on short-term programs with SAMS or the Diocese of Haiti, retirees have gone on to spend their "golden years" in sharing themselves and their skills with people who can benefit from their experience.

When short-term missioners return home, their world has been turned upside down. Very often these missionaries go out again and again at their own expense. It is out of such experiences that "world Christians" are born and, persuaded and inspired by their vision, their parishes and dioceses begin to catch fire.

All these exciting developments have animated the work of the Task Force to Re-Vision the Domestic and Foreign Missionary Society. When it reports back at the General Convention in Philadelphia in 1997, the burden of its message will be that the goal of the church is to enable Episcopalians to be involved as supporters, witnesses, and people of prayer in proclaiming Christ by word and deed to the ends of the earth. This goal is best achieved by a network of bodies—official and unofficial; local, diocesan, and national; Anglican and ecumenical—rather than any centrally controlled program. Furthermore, this should happen within the context of a whole church which could deliberately turn itself into a "network of networks," each component of which stands or falls on the basis of its vision and its support from the grassroots.[10]

Sharing our faith to the ends of the earth is still considered a questionable, even disreputable, undertaking by many because they have either not taken the time or had the opportunity to see how much the whole concept of mission has been changing. Mission today and tomorrow takes place from everywhere to everywhere, and as we have noticed already, in the years ahead we could well find ourselves receiving as many missioners as we send out. Our present structures are in transition toward enabling Episcopalians to share in this two-way global mission more effectively. We Americans may still have the lion's share of material resources and like to flex our muscles accordingly, but the task ahead is to see how what we bring to the table can be coordinated with the skills and vivacity our partners in Zaire or Uruguay can bring. One of the challenges ahead of us is to welcome Anglicans from overseas as involved players in the life of our church, rather than as interesting, but very temporary, visitors. To date, we have not really been prepared to listen to the

---

10. Richard Kew is a member of this task force, established by Resolution #DO16, which is made up of equal numbers of members of the SCWM and ECGM.

critique of teams from other parts of the Communion in the two Partners in Mission consultations the Episcopal Church has participated in. We are sorry to say that there is little reason to believe we have yet developed the necessary humility to sit at their feet and learn from them as we enter the new millennium.[11]

∞ *Looking Toward Tomorrow*

Between now and 2015 one of our highest priorities must be to teach and inspire Episcopalians to fulfill their baptismal promise "to proclaim by word and example the Good News of God in Christ" to the ends of the earth. None of us has a right to be excused from this obligation, and with ingenuity and dedication we still have both the people and resources to be a valuable player on the world Christian scene. If we fail to act, we may find ourselves not being taken seriously, while depriving ourselves of vital opportunities for spiritual growth. We have the will to make considerable change when it really matters. A generation ago, for example, we had one of the weakest stewardship records in the mainline churches; today our figures are among the best. It took vision, theological understanding, and hard work to ensure that a growing proportion of our parishes take the stewardship of time, treasure and talent very seriously.

The same can be true for world mission. It is perfectly possible for the Episcopal Church to develop some of the most exciting and visionary global ministries in the world during the next twenty years. Unencumbered by yesterday's structures, we will be free to experiment with approaches that are unconventional and could work wonderfully because, as business consultant Tom Peters says, "Crazy times require crazy solutions." We are blessed

---

11. Since the gathering Mutual Responsibility and Interdependence (MRI), held in Canada in the 1960s, the Partners in Mission consultation process has enabled provinces of the Anglican Communion to open themselves up to input from fellow Anglicans from elsewhere in the world. ECUSA has hosted two since then, but while some far-reaching suggestions were made, few have been acted upon.

with gifted people, abundant resources, and rich reservoirs of imagination and creativity. Like the world, the global church is changing so rapidly that missionary partnership in tomorrow's world will be very different from anything we have known in the past.

In the years ahead, it is clear that God is calling us from narrowness and parochialism to global involvement. Not only does this enable us to share our blessings, it will bring health to our churches too! Through these developing networks the challenge is going to be made to dioceses, local congregations, and emerging coalitions of committed people to take the initiative for themselves. This call will be visionary, life-transforming, and sacrificial, for the harvest is plentiful, but the laborers are few.

Summary

- Episcopalians have a limited grasp of the global extent of the church, being prone to think and act locally. At the same time, we fear being labeled "imperialists" if we venture outside our own culture with the message of Christ.

- We are members of a dynamic, worldwide communion whose center of gravity is the global South.

- The "third wave" of the quantum, or information, age is sweeping the world, challenging all received structures and interconnecting all of us.

- In a fast-changing and troubled world, our message is that in Christ God's kingdom is in our midst. Our mission needs to be constantly renewed and reconceived.

- Mission is a two-way street. North America is also a mission field for others. Episcopalians have not always had the humility and grace to receive missioners as partners in mission.

QUESTIONS FOR DISCUSSION

- Make a list of reasons why the Episcopal Church has been so globally disengaged, and discuss why you think we prefer to take care of ourselves. How does such global disengagement in mission manifest itself in your parish?

- Are we embarrassed by the words of John 14:6, "I am the way, the truth, and the life"? What do you think Jesus meant by these words?

- How are radically transformed telecommunications and computers changing your view of the world?

- What are the primary tensions in the world? Do you think we are heading for a world in which it is "the rest against the West"? How should this view change our approach to global ministry?

- Imagine how your parish would use a missionary from some other part of the world to enable you to fulfill your mission.

- Discuss four things you might do to help your parish be more conscious of and involved in global mission.

- What is the relationship between prayer and being "world Christians"?

9

The Ecumenical Wild Card

If the challenge confronting the church in the realm of mission is the broadening of our horizons in order to think and act globally, in the field of ecumenical relations the real dynamics are at the grassroots level. For too long we have left the mechanics of our ecumenical involvement in the hands of theologians, bishops, and bureaucrats who confer both nationally and internationally. While these conversations have not been without significant fruit, they have tended to be removed from local congregations.

One example of this approach to ecumenism is the *rapprochement* between the Episcopal Church and the Evangelical Lutheran Church of America (ELCA). During the last twenty years, we have steadily been moving toward an agreement—a Concordat—which could eventually lead us to full communion with one another, and may be initiated as early as 1997. While there are generally good relationships between Episcopal and Lutheran congregations at the parish level, for the most part the clergy and laity in both denominations have been out of the loop; they know little about what is happening with the agreement, and how it might affect their lives. Yet here is the paradox: once the agreement is signed and sealed, it will be left in their hands to turn this vision into a reality.

As we look back in history, there has always been a close relationship between effective mission and Christian unity. The ecumenical movement sprang from the growing realization of the Victorian churches that if they were to evangelize the world in their generation, then it was essential that different Christian traditions be seen as sisters and brothers in Christ, not representatives of competing religions. It seems to us that there has to be a functional purpose behind Christian cooperation and intercommunion if ecumenism is to have any real meaning and thus to fulfill the mission of the church.

One of the great temptations as we look at ecumenism is to be cynical. On the one hand, some "ecumaniacs" seem to be into unity merely for unity's sake. On the other hand, there are many who share one Lutheran bishop's perspective as he wondered aloud if movements toward some kind of unification with the Episcopal Church are little more than two ailing old-line denominations getting into bed together in order to keep each other warm while they die.

We do not share such skepticism. Not only are the indications good that the Concordat will be passed comfortably by the national governing conventions of the two churches in mid-1997, there are signs that such a movement could very well enhance the mission of the church in the long term. We have noticed that one of the pressures upon the churches in England, as secularization has made the environment ever more indifferent, even hostile toward religious faith, has been for Christians to deepen their relationships with one another across denominational divides. We expect the same dynamics to prevail among increasing numbers of churches in North America as our society begins to equal Europe's level of secularity.

∽ *A Broadening of the Base*
Until recently, the two major ecumenical dialogues in which the Episcopal Church has been involved have been with the Lutherans and the Roman Catholics, internationally, nationally, at state and at local levels. This configuration is beginning to change as

the United Methodist Church moves toward being one of the players, turning this from a three-way to a four-way relationship. This represents a fascinating change of direction for the Methodists, who had thought until now that Anglicans really were not willing to take them seriously on the ecumenical stage. Furthermore, change is taking place within Methodism. It is interesting that at the 1996 General Conference of the United Methodist Church several resolutions passed which hinted a greater commitment on the part of Methodists to ecumenical relations and the affirmation of a more historical, sacramental theology. Furthermore, we both have Methodist friends who tell us that within Methodism in the United States there are many who are beginning to reexplore their Anglican roots.

Until fairly recently, Methodism was the largest Protestant body in the United States. Early in this century, the denominations that preceded today's United Methodist Church made up nearly one-quarter of all church memberships in this country. There was, perhaps, within Methodism the sense that they did not need close ecumenical relationships with anyone else. This is obviously now changing quite radically, and we look forward to the continued and deeper participation of John Wesley's spiritual children in this great movement for mission and unity.

Ecumenical relations among the mainline liturgical churches appear the most encouraging and the most predictable. As we look out across the rest of the ecumenical landscape, however, very little else is as clear. If we were talking about a card game, ecumenism would certainly be the wild card, the joker. It is not all that difficult to identify the direction many of the trends are taking us these days, but most things ecumenical are fraught with far too many imponderables.

Our unwillingness to predict the direction of ecumenism in the coming millennium illustrates some of the confusion and malaise at the heart of traditional models of moving toward Christian unity. While certain Christian traditions are working toward closer cooperation with each other, some old-line congregations are splintering off to join different, often newer, denominations.

As far as North American Anglicans are concerned, the Charismatic Episcopal Church, an amalgam of former Episcopalians, Pentecostals, and others, is the best known of several cases in point. Could it be that such fragmentation will accelerate, and that this process is one of the initial steps in a much larger realignment of the nation's denominations? We illustrate this ecclesiastical disintegration using an Episcopal example, but something similar is happening in most other traditions.

Meanwhile, relationships among different religious traditions at the congregational level are stronger than ever. Celebratory, evangelistic, and educational activities involving a variety of denominations are multifold, often encouraged by parachurch organizations. This crossfertilization, in turn, makes it much easier for Christians to switch from one religious tradition to another when they find themselves out of sympathy or disgruntled with their current parish—a reflection that traditional denominational loyalties are eroding, and that believers, as religious consumers, want a whole supermarket of choices. Some lay Christians have "church-shopped" for years; now, as those born after 1955 begin reaching their middle years, this phenomenon has increased sharply.

A new twist to this is that now the clergy are joining in. Not only are pastors leaving one congregation to serve another in the same denomination, they are also transferring to other denominations or nondenominational situations. Furthermore, in certain circumstances, when pastors find their convictions changing or when they fall out of sympathy with their present denomination and change allegiances, some have been able to take most of their flock with them into the new tradition.

This trend is further strengthened by the fact that some denominations are actively recruiting both clergy and congregations. While we are tempted to identify this trend solely with the newer and more media-savvy Christian bodies, such as the Evangelical Episcopal Church, actually one of the most successful proponents of this approach has been the ancient Antiochian Orthodox Church, the tradition within Orthodoxy that has worked the hardest to Americanize itself. They have managed to recruit both clergy and parishes, and have for a number of years targeted the Episcopal Church as one of their most attractive sources for new members.

This wave of church shopping by laity, increasing numbers of clergy, and denominations looking for new congregations reveals a novel ecclesiastical environment in the United States. All churches, whether they are members of old-line denominations like the Episcopal Church or have no formal affiliation at all, are competing passionately with one another for the next generation of churchgoers and Christians. Add to this the fact that the church is no longer the first place people look to have their spiritual needs met, and the competition is only going to get more intense during the years ahead.[1]

These changing circumstances illustrate the complexity of the ecumenical challenge as the Episcopal Church moves into the new millennium. Not only do we have various Christian denominations seeking out our disaffected members and "preying" upon us, we must also find ways to rebuild relationships with those who have decided to leave us—or who have left already. In the years ahead we have our work cut out building bridges to those who consider themselves to be Anglican but have either walked out of communion with us, or have chosen to be Anglican but to remain outside this fold. This is not necessarily going to be an easy task, because family disputes are often more difficult to resolve than those with friends or strangers. In addition, the non-canonical Anglicans represent a broad array of theological tastes and ecclesiastical sympathies.

---

1. This phenomenon is talked about at some length by Lyle E. Schaller in many of his writings. See, for example, *The New Reformation* (Nashville: Abingdon, 1995) and *Tattered Trust: Is There Hope for Your Denomination?* (Nashville: Abingdon, 1996).

✑ Other Wild Cards

While the United Methodists are becoming more accepting of institutional ecumenism, voting at their 1996 General Conference to begin moving toward full union with a variety of traditions, most other denominations who have been part of the movement appear only lukewarm. The Episcopal Church is no different from the majority in this instance. Vehicles like the Consultation on Church Union (COCU) can be perceived either as the last gasp of moves toward organic unity by churches in a survival mode, or as an opportunity for all of them to focus upon the true meaning of God's mission. Our hunch is that the former of these options is more likely to be true.

Perhaps one major reason denominational union appears to be floundering is that within most of the participating traditions irreconcilable internal conflicts rage, diverting attention and energy. Many observers have noted that the issue facing these Christian bodies is not so much the differences among them as the differences *within* their traditions. Some of these differences are focused on issues of sexuality in the life of the church, but increasing numbers on the theologically "progressive" end of the spectrum also want after a millennium and a half to reopen the debate on creedal matters, such as the nature of the Holy Trinity. These conflicts rage irrespective of the convictions and sensibilities of the vast majority in the middle.

There is a possibility that in the Episcopal Church, as in all these other denominations, a reinvigorated center committed to the proclamation of the gospel together with Christian service and action could reassert itself, but this appears less likely with the passing of time. While it might be impossible to bring together the extremes of left and right, it is likely that the whole shape of denominations will change, or be forced to change, radically. As sociologist William McKinney asserts, "This is the time for some old churches to think some new thoughts."

Another wild card in the deck is the emergence of a broad cross-section of evangelical, charismatic, and nondenominational churches, which have become ever more prominent in a great number of cities and suburbs during the last fifteen or twenty years. While not necessarily prickly toward those in the traditional denominations, these congregations have sprung from a source which tends to shun cooperation with others, especially those whose theological or ecclesiological heritage they believe to be suspect. While some of these congregations emerge and die down within one generation, the majority are likely to live for a long time, and so may, during the second generation, recognize their need to be part of a larger whole that can enhance their work and offer a network which provides a broader environment for their ongoing ministry.

It is interesting that Willow Creek Church in Barrington, Illinois, perhaps the most publicized of these independent megachurches in recent years, has established an affiliation for similar congregations in order to provide fellowship for pastors and lay leaders, and a network of support which almost all congregations discover they eventually need. We find it fascinating that the fast-growing Vineyard Fellowship of Churches has now established regional leaders with responsibilities very similar to those of an Episcopal bishop or other old-line church judicatory executives. We gather that their commissioning was even based upon the service for the consecration of bishops in the *Book of Common Prayer!*

Despite their apparent numerical success, leading evangelical thinkers are voicing increasing concern over the superficiality of the more conservative tradition in American Christianity. We have noticed already that evangelical scholars deplore the hollowing out of their theological foundations. Thoughtful conservative Christians as a whole are increasingly uncomfortable with the sentimentality and shallowness of their environment, and continue to explore the rootedness of mainline Christianity, especially those traditions with a liturgical and sacramental life for which so many of them yearn. It is not surprising that, unwilling to join themselves to comprehensive denominations like our own, they are attempting to recreate similar structures for mutual oversight and support within their own theological framework.

We are excited by much of what is happening in this broadly evangelical and charismatic tradition, though we ourselves cannot endorse all that they say and do. The old-line churches tend to become defensive and stand-offish when it comes to developing relationships with such congregations; some refuse even to enter into conversation with them. We are the poorer for it, and we rob them of access to the treasures of our own rich Anglicanism.

Yet another variable is the dramatic decline of confidence in the major conciliar entities, the National and the World Council of Churches. This is reflected in the diminished funding flowing to each of these bodies from the old-line denominations. They are perceived as not having focused on matters of faith and order, but appear to have given themselves over to a host of cooperative ventures that have often been at odds with the convictions of many at the grassroots of their member churches, the ones who ultimately pay the bills. Alongside this has been an apparent watering down of Christian distinctives. These factors have compromised the ability of the NCC and WCC to remain major players in moves toward Christian unity.

We have painted a picture of a changing ecclesiastical scene in the United States, and that fluidity is likely to continue as far as we can see into the future. Such messiness is the inevitable outcome of churches attempting to function in the midst of a major historical transformation. It is impossible to see how the process will play itself out in the next twenty years, and how this broad array of churches will react. There are just too many wild cards in the pack, and even if we could predict what might happen in the Episcopal Church, there is no telling what might happen in other denominations—or nondenominations. Whichever way you look at it, major restructuring of denominational traditions appears almost inevitable. The question is when and how.

∞ *The International Scene*

While on the whole there is a slow thaw in relations between the churches in the East and the West, these relationships are clearly volatile, with many ups and downs. As recently as 1994 we thought we perceived on the part of Pope John Paul II an eagerness to bridge the gap between Rome and Orthodoxy, even in his own lifetime. Yet relations between East and West have been made more difficult by the recent establishment of Roman Catholic structures in Russia, and an unexpected strain in relations between Rome and Constantinople during the last few years.

A further complicating factor is the fractiousness within Orthodoxy, which has appeared a potential partner for deepening ecumenical relations to Anglicanism. Orthodoxy seems at the moment fraught with internal difficulties and power plays. The emergence of a reinvigorated post-Soviet Russian Orthodox Church has inevitably upset the balance of power in inter-Orthodox relationships. This has recently been illustrated by a barely averted schism between the Patriarchs of Moscow and Constantinople over whose sphere of influence the Estonian Orthodox Church might fall into. The cracks of this divide were papered over in the summer of 1996, but the tensions remain.

Vatican watchers are already discussing possible successors to Pope John Paul II, who has appeared to age considerably during the mid-1990s. There is no telling what a change in the papacy could bring forth. A forward-looking pope could initiate a new cordiality among all the churches, but one who is reactionary or defensive could bring ecumenism to a lurching halt, and even throw the engine into reverse. The papacy is yet another wild card in the ecumenical game.

Perhaps the proposed Concordat between the Episcopal Church and the ELCA, or the Porvoo agreement in Europe between the Anglican and Lutheran Churches there, could become models for deepening relationships with other Protestant denominations, eventually leading to full communion. We assume that the Concordat and the Porvoo agreement have laid a foundation for global intercommunion and eventually full fellowship between the Anglican Communion and the Worldwide Lutheran Federation.

While the whole ecumenical endeavor seems to be in the midst of as much transition as its participating churches, there are occasional signs of hope on the horizon. For example, a work by German Catholic theologians Heinrich Fries and Karl Rahner entitled *Unity of Churches: An Actual Possibility* presents a grassroots approach to ecumenism that fits well with the prevailing mood within the churches and our culture. Ideas like these can breathe new life into the lagging ecumenical conversation.

Fries and Rahner believe that the unity of the church is far too important a subject to leave in the hands of theologians, bishops, and bureaucrats. These theologians begin with the implication that the mission of the church should be the top priority; our union should be in the service of that mission. Starting with realistic assumptions, they abandon many of the utopian premises that have marred the ecumenical dialogue in the past, and then go on to speak of what is actually possible. The eight theses Fries and Rahner propose have shocked many Catholics and astounded many Protestants, for they ask that in this aggressively secular age we suspend discussion of the many relatively minor differences that separate our various ecclesial bodies, and instead focus on our common ground and common goal: "We come from the same stock, and we are moving toward the same end, and in the interim we have these differences." By laying aside our differences and attempting to move together toward this common goal, we find might ourselves becoming obedient to the will of our Lord—which is the unity of his people, "for Christ alone frees us from bondage to the limitations of our own history, and opens up new channels of experience on the way to the one church of the future."[2] Could it be that a consensus will emerge around such ideas, and that the mission of God has to be primary in our search for unity? Such an approach holds out much more hope than a unity that seeks to "cluster" traditions organically, thus continuing the tired old denominational paradigm.

---

2. Heinrich Fries and Karl Rahner, *Unity of Churches: An Actual Possibility* (Philadelphia: Fortress, 1988).

∞ The Future of Ecumenism

It would seem that the spirit of our age stands against future hopes for Christian union. The ecumenical movement as we know it grew up at a time when one of the dominant motifs in western culture was that of convergence. At the same time that the World Council of Churches was inaugurated, the United Nations was also coming into being, and soon afterward the European Community. The times in which we live are very different. We live in an age where divergence has become a predominant motif.

Rather than drawing entities together in some organic whole, networks are becoming the means whereby we retain our autonomy while working in cooperation with others. Could this be the prevailing pattern for interdenominational Christian activity in the years ahead? Could it be that as we move toward 2015 creative approaches toward networking at the grassroots will become the means by which a new style of ecumenism finds its way forward? From our present perspective, we can only guess.

What we can assert is that enthusiasm about reunion among the traditional denominations has, by and large, dissipated for the time being. Energies have been internalized. Denominations are now focusing upon their own concerns, their own inner conflicts, and their own survival. We cannot expect significant leadership moving toward reunion during the foreseeable future.

The retired presiding bishop of the ELCA, addressing its conference of bishops not long ago, focused the domestic issues of America's mainline churches when he asked the question, "Whither denominations?" He pointed up the fact that almost all of them are struggling with finances, shrinking membership, and some kind of reorganization. All are wrestling with the question, "What is the future of denominations in America?" Given this set of wild cards, alongside differing local, national, and international circumstances, we are certain that during the next two decades our whole approach to ecumenical dialogue and activity is bound to undergo a radical change.

SUMMARY

- Ecumenical relationships really begin at the parish level rather than at the national level.

- The Episcopal-Lutheran Concordat is one of the few concrete achievements on an otherwise unimpressive ecumenical scene.

- The United Methodist Church is awakening to significant ecumenical involvement.

- There is considerable unpredictability on the ecumenical scene, with a fluidity of movement among denominations by individuals, clergy, and whole congregations.

- For a number of reasons it is not easy to build bridges with former Episcopalians.

- We have not worked hard enough at developing relationships with nondenominational congregations.

- There is a diminishing role by the National and World Council of Churches, and great volatility on the international scene.

- What is actually possible at the grassroots could provide ecumenical hope in the future.

- In previous generations convergence was the dominant motif; today, it is divergence.

QUESTIONS FOR DISCUSSION

- What does your parish know about the Lutheran-Episcopal Concordat? How do you think it is going to influence your church life?

- Are you aware of any formal agreements among Episcopalians, Roman Catholics, Lutherans, and United Methodists, locally or statewide? If you are, what difference are the agreements making to the way you exercise your ministry?

- Have you tried getting to know nondenominational churches in your community? If so, what have you learned? If not, how can you establish such relationships, and what do you think you would benefit from them?

- What do you think are the greatest challenges as we try to reconnect with former Episcopalians who have joined another denomination or a non-canonical Anglican church?

- Study John 17:1-26. What do you think is the relationship between the unity of God and the unity of Christians?

- What could you achieve with other local churches to enhance the proclamation of the gospel?

10

Reformation, Fragmentation, or Just Muddling Along?

Whatever Martin Luther's motives were when he nailed his "Ninety-Five Theses upon Indulgences" to the door of the castle church in Wittenberg on the eve of All Saints, 1517, he could not have imagined the chain of events that simple action would set in motion. He thought he was inviting scholarly debate: his theses were propositions from one theologian to be weighed by other theologians. However, what set Luther apart was that he wrote from his heart as much as his head, and he was expressing the yearnings of ordinary people as well as presenting a theological dilemma. As such, historian Owen Chadwick wrote, his condemnation of the system of indulgences "echoed the cry of the German people against Italian exactions."[1] Luther's scholarly challenge struck a popular chord, and was printed and rapidly distributed across Germany.

---

1. Owen Chadwick, *The Reformation* (Harmondsworth, England: Penguin Books, 1964), p. 43.

For years, Luther had immersed himself in the thought of Paul and Augustine. His intensive study of the letter to the Romans had evoked a profound experience of God's grace, which forced him to realize how poorly the contemporary church measured up against its apostolic forerunner and led him to long for the *restoration* of a church now badly marred by theological error and corruption. This miner's son probably set in motion the torrent of *reformation* almost by accident!

Reformers, whoever they are and whenever they live, seldom set out to tear down existing structures. Frequently they are so shocked by the forces they unleash that, like Luther, they then attempt to slow down what they first set in motion. Yet once reform begins, it gathers momentum, takes on a life of its own, and is unlikely to decelerate appreciably until its objectives have been fulfilled. As we look back on the first Reformation, we cannot but be amazed at the speed with which it swept all before it, and how it "cleansed"—while fragmenting—the western church. In a couple of generations European religion was turned upside down.

Something similar is happening today, and as it accelerates, it carries all before it. This chapter asks how our denominational structures will stand up as the tectonic plates shift beneath our feet and hurricane-force winds howl in our ears. The ideas that follow have, of necessity, a strongly impressionistic flavor from within the midst of the surge of events and wild intensity of the crosscurrents.

∞ The Seeds of Change are Germinating

In *New Millennium, New Church* we predicted that a major transition taking place within our culture would rapidly steer us away from hierarchies to patterns of interlocking networks. We indicated that this would profoundly affect the Episcopal Church. This process is now in full swing.

At that time a new generation of leaders, uneasy with a line-of-command approach to organization, was starting to displace the older generation, and we sensed these new leaders would be uncomfortable with pyramidic structures. We are now well into this transition, and wherever these younger leaders stand on the theological, political, or cultural spectrum, it is apparent most have limited patience with, or investment in, many long-standing church structures. While seldom talked about, differences in the generations is one of many undercurrents of tension within the church. The reality is that anyone born after 1950 to 1955 is going to think very differently from someone born before that period. This same tension exists in the wider culture: although there are various factors coloring the distrust that many older citizens have toward President Clinton, for example, generational differences play a major role.

Given the changes in society, the trend toward networks, and this generational shift, we suggested in *New Millennium, New Church* that the modest national structural reforms—including the move to relocate the Episcopal Church's national headquarters to Kansas City that was blocked by General Convention in the eighties—would pale beside the radical and even iconoclastic solutions of the nineties. Our observations have been on target: the church is in the midst of a tug-of-war which will ultimately result in an abandonment of familiar but dated configurations that owe more to pre- and postwar business practices and culture than to God's mission, the Scriptures, and our historic apostolic order. The different perceptions of younger generations and the emerging era's approach to information is forcing Christian organizations to restructure themselves, transforming them from hierarchical chains of command into organic networks and systems that are much more compatible with Paul's image of the church as the Body of Christ, with every member linked to every other member and the whole dependent on Christ.

Again and again in this book we have asserted that the local congregation is the frontline of the church's mission. This means that while the diocese, if configured appropriately, has a significant role to play in providing support for ministry at the grassroots, huge structures over and above that are no longer necessary.

Our present structures are built hierarchically and vertically, from the top down. Lyle Schaller writes:

> Systems built on vertical lines naturally tend to urge, "Send us money and people so we can do what you cannot do." That naturally creates a self-fulfilling prophecy—denominational systems are needed to do what congregations and regional judicatories do not know how to do or cannot be trusted to do.[2]

We live in an era of networks, and managing an interlocking web of networks requires a very different approach to organization, control, and therefore to leadership. Two of the leading gurus of networking assert, "The nature of control changes with widespread communication and knowledge. Local decision-making combines with centralized information sharing in the 'network-enabled' hierarchy."[3]

We have seen already that local congregations usually bypass established structures as they search out resources for ministry. Parishes seldom consider what, if anything, the denomination has to offer, but go directly to any number of agencies and publishers—both within and beyond Anglicanism—for help with their work.[4] Today's national structures are crumbling not only because they were designed for an utterly different world, but also because they were geared for a world which handled information, people, and resources in radically different ways. Furthermore, the very

---

2. Lyle Schaller, *Tattered Trust: Is There Hope for Your Denomination?* (Nashville: Abingdon, 1996), p. 44.

3. Jessica Lipnack and Jeffrey Stamps, *The Age of Networks* (Essex Junction, VT: Omneo, 1994), p. 43.

4. One interesting illustration of this happened in Murfreesboro, Tennessee, in July 1996, when a large Southern Baptist congregation and the Episcopal parish had their Vacation Bible Schools in successive weeks. Neither was using denominational materials, but each was using the identical curriculum produced by the same independent publisher. Another is the *Journey to Adulthood* formation process for teenagers developed by Amanda Hughes and David Crean, which began in the Episcopal Church but is already being adopted and adapted to suit the needs of several other denominations.

existence of some of these structures diverts precious resources away from the grassroots, the primary *locus* of ministry.

Tomorrow's structures have to be both horizontal and adaptable if they are to deliver on mission. Church leaders are disposed toward maintaining the status quo, which has resulted in a top-heavy national organization headed by a Presiding Bishop whose job description is more like that of CEO than a pastor. It is time that the office of Presiding Bishop, like that of the Archbishop of Canterbury, once again include some form of continuing diocesan oversight, as it did prior to World War II.

If the Presiding Bishop's primary task was to maintain a link with his or her diocese, preside over the House of Bishops, represent the Episcopal Church ecumenically and in the worldwide Anglican Communion, and provide pastoral support for a divided and pummeled episcopate, that would be more than enough for one person to do. Such an alteration would require certain canonical changes, and the provision by the slimmed-down national structures of resources to permit a suffragan, coadjutor, or assistant bishop to handle much of the day-to-day administration of the Presiding Bishop's diocese, as is the case in the archepiscopal dioceses of York and Canterbury. But it would not require an extensive church staff headquartered in Manhattan.

∞ Whither Denominations?

Most of the thinking being done about the shape of the future church presupposes stability and the maintenance of the kind of church we have now. It assumes that the Episcopal Church's inherited structures will retain most of their present contours. Yet to think this way is to whistle into the wind. Half a millennium ago totally new structures were needed to contain the "new wine" of the Reformation; using these structures, the gospel was taken to the ends of the earth.[5] A centuries-long process has now run

---

5. Perhaps the most brilliant analysis of this process is found in the chapters on Reformation, Enlightenment, and Post-Enlightenment mission in David Bosch's *Transforming Mission* (Maryknoll, NY: Orbis, 1991).

its course and today's denominations are trapped, with nowhere to go. "Decades of denial," writes Leonard Sweet, "have created in the church 'major messes.'...Problems have metastasized, infecting the entire system."[6] Even as late as 1993 we imagined that the Episcopal Church—and most other old-line denominations, for that matter—would somehow hold together, if only out of habit, nostalgia, or the loyalty of clergy to pension funds! Most looked as if they could muddle through, yet with each passing month, this seems less likely. Could it be that issues of sexuality in the church will play the catalytic role that indulgences did in toppling the medieval church?

While the apostolic continuities embodied in Anglicanism have a growing attraction for tens of thousands, and will continue to thrive, most of the edifices that have housed them are fast becoming archaeological curiosities. What Loren Mead dubbed the "Christendom paradigm" gave us today's denominations; many of us have yet to notice that it ran out of steam a while back. Something new is stirring. The potent new wine of the gospel *must* have fresh wineskins if it is to free Christians to be faithful in the future.

We are crossing a hinge of history. The Russian novelist Alexander Solzhenitsyn maintains that "if the world has not approached its end, it has reached a major watershed in history equal in importance to the turn of the Middle Ages to the Renaissance."[7] Just as the upheavals of that era resulted in a massive refitting of the church, the emerging Quantum Age calls forth something similar. Loren Mead writes:

> In such a world it is hard to keep one's bearings....I do not expect clarity about the new church for several generations—I shall not see it, even though I work for it. That is true for most of us, I think. But perhaps there may be some of the young

---

6. Leonard Sweet, *FaithQuakes* (Nashville: Abingdon, 1994), p. 12.
7. Alexander Solzhenitsyn, *A World Split Apart* (New York: Harper and Row, 1978), p. 61.

among us who will, like Moses, be led up to the high mountain from which at least to see the Promised Land.[8]

As uncomfortable as it might be, Mead is right to urge us to think in the very long term: we are only at the front end of this gigantic transition.

∞ Arrivals, Departures, Mergers, Alliances

Just as the Reformation of the sixteenth century had its radicals, moderates, and conservatives, the same is true today, with every voice loud, shrill, and determined to be heard. As Christians grapple with today's dilemmas, a variety of structural ideas with their accompanying theological rationales is appearing. We are even trying on some for size. As in the sixteenth century, so in the twenty-first: when churches reconfigure there are bound to be painful partings. The most bruising separations are likely to take place between Christians in the old-line denominations because they accommodate the broadest array of theological perceptions, and are already stressed by the deepest antagonisms.

If divisions take place, they are unlikely to be clean breaks between two polar factions who then attempt to coax those in the middle to tag along. A process of fragmentation and splintering appears more likely. Congregations and individuals are already washing their hands of the old structures, and there are enough antagonisms and contending coalitions to turn the process into an ongoing nightmare. How this might happen is anyone's guess, but the carcass of today's church will be picked clean by splinter groups until little is left. If this happens in one denomination then we may see a "domino effect" as the others disintegrate in turn. From the morass of fragments that are left over, new alliances would ultimately form, and from these will emerge new ways of being the church.

---

8. Loren Mead, *The Once and Future Church* (Washington, D.C.: The Alban Institute, 1991), pp. 84-85.

If you think we are straying into the realms of science fiction, reflect upon the pent-up fluidity across the spectrum of American Christianity. A rash of ecclesiastical migrations and shifts is taking place as denominations, as institutions, reach the crisis point. "Brand-name loyalty is dying," says one Cooperative Baptist Fellowship leader, itself a "church within the church" we know as the Southern Baptist Convention. Another observer notes that "in two hundred years, this is the most serious transition denominations have gone through....Some people are calling this the post-denominational age. We are in an in-between time, and we don't know what we're going to end up with."[9]

Individual parishes in the Episcopal Church have already headed off to newly-formed Anglican churches, while Roman Catholic and nondenominational congregations have affiliated with the Episcopal Church. Southern Baptists have joined the charismatic Vineyard Fellowship, while one Vineyard congregation has made a journey to the Antiochian Orthodox Church at the opposite end of the spectrum. Like the Evangelical Episcopal Church created in October 1995, the Antiochians have been advertising for congregations who might join them.[10]

Elsewhere, the United Church of Christ in various places has shown signs of dissolving as an identifiable tradition altogether. So significant are the numbers of churches divorcing themselves from one ecclesial family in favor of another that this phenomenon caught the eye of the *Wall Street Journal:*

> Throughout non-Catholic Christianity, churches are being born again, especially among independent churches. Even among some centralized denominations, the switch is occur-

---

9. Professor William Leonard, Chair of Religion, Sanford University, Birmingham, Alabama, reported in *The Dayton Daily News* (March 6, 1996).

10. The Evangelical Episcopal Church was formed in Fredericksburg, Virginia, in October 1995, and by June 1996 already had 210 congregations. Michael Owen, their presiding bishop, suggested that "his church is part of a 'convergence movement' comprised of evangelicals seeking to find 'roots' by adopting historic liturgy and creeds." (*Religion Watch* [July-August, 1996].)

ring. There are Baptist churches becoming Presbyterian, Lutheran churches going charismatic, Pentecostal churches turning Episcopal and so on. The number of denominational switches reaches well into the hundreds, and religious experts say the pace is accelerating.[11]

As an older denomination which has for centuries been at the heart of American life, the Episcopal Church is perhaps even more vulnerable to reconfiguration than more recent and homogeneous arrivals.

∽ The End of Episcopal Loyalties

In our first book we commented on the loyalty of Episcopalians, a quality envied by Christians of less delible hues. As the nineties have progressed, however, disgruntlement and the post-denominational character of the age have soured Episcopalians, dissolving this fidelity for many. Erosion has been abetted by scandals, coupled with a sense at the grassroots that many church leaders, clergy and lay, are interested more in control than helping the local church be a "colony of heaven" (see Philippians 3:20) in the midst of an increasingly hostile culture. Furthermore, the issues which seem to preoccupy most leaders appear irrelevant to younger Boomers and Generation Xers in the church, and their style turns them off altogether. Lyle Schaller points out that "younger generations and new immigrants tend not to be attracted to any institution that is organized on the principle that people cannot be trusted"—which is to say, institutions that devalue the laity and the grassroots in favor of maintaining what is already in place.[12]

The rising generation stands in stark contrast to their elders, who dominated the church until recently. Their attention spans and fuses are shorter, and they will not hang around if they think the church does not trust them, or is heading in the wrong

---

11. *The Wall Street Journal* (May 1996), article by Calmetta Y. Coleman.
12. Schaller, *Tattered Trust*, p. 52.

direction and they are powerless to do anything about it. Yet the institutional church continues to deny what is occurring in its midst. As Kevin Martin, Canon for Congregational Development in the Episcopal Diocese of Texas, has said, "The longer lifespan of the 'George Bush' generation, combined with their institutional loyalty, combined with their generosity toward the church, has created an atmosphere of denial that predominates in our institutional life."

For more than a generation too many leaders have shrugged off our numerical slippage. This habit, often coupled with justifying theologies, or defensiveness in the face of apparent failure, has been a key facet of institutional denial. Yet whether we are losing individuals to secularity, New Age superstitions, or the disaffiliation of congregations in favor of other denominations, what results is the institutional equivalent of an overweight and middle-aged businessman ignoring the warning signs of his body that he is on the verge of coronary shut-down. Worrying over temporary dips in the statistics might amount to hypochondria on the part of the church, but ignoring thirty years of unbroken decline is to deny that the pain in your head comes from the endless bashing you are getting from a two-by-four!

Although encouraging developments can be seen in many places, morale and enthusiasm are generally low and the church is mired in a dizzying cycle of controversies which absorb energy and divert our attention at the precise moment that spiritual awareness and longing are on the increase in the wider culture. Indications are that the harvest is riper than it has been for decades, but the Episcopal Church is just not looking, and thus appears uninterested. Furthermore, while younger voices are suggesting the Episcopal Church is blessed with almost everything they are looking for, they have little or no time for a self-centered, self-absorbed church that merely reflects contemporary American cultural norms—they seek authenticity.

In talking with those who have left, it seems that what causes their departure is a variety of troublesome issues which disturb and accumulate until, finally, the last straw is dropped on the camel's back. At that point they throw up their hands and leave, and nothing can persuade them to reconsider. They often experience elation in the period immediately following departure, like the release felt by someone leaving a bad marriage; later, agony over what might have been settles in. Just as the elderly John Henry Newman, then a cardinal of the Church of Rome, entertained a wistfulness for his Anglican past, a similar wistfulness remains in the hearts of many who have departed this fold.

All sorts of reasons are given for leaving. Here are just some of the more prevalent from the last few years:

- Dislike of the positions taken by church leaders, whether they are too "conservative" or too "liberal."
- Dislike of specific views on sexuality: either the Episcopal Church is sexually too inclusive, prepared to accept and ordain non-celibate homosexuals too readily, *or* it is utterly homophobic, with gay and lesbian people persecuted and denied full participation.
- The structures of the Episcopal Church are perceived to be secretive and corrupt, as seen by the scandal of Ellen Cooke, former treasurer of the church, who embezzled at least $2.2 million of the church's money.
- The Episcopal Church has drifted away from its theological moorings. It no longer takes Scripture or its apostolic traditions seriously, and it is reluctant to reflect theologically before it acts and speaks.
- There are too many forces in the Episcopal Church who are unwilling to explore the theological boundaries, who are mired in "fundamentalism," and who refuse to take seriously liberal scholarship, the findings of the social and human sciences, or the emergence of women and minorities.
- This church should not ordain women to the priesthood.
- The Episcopal Church is too lax on issues surrounding the sanctity of life. The church seems utterly insensitive to those concerned about either abortion or euthanasia.[13]

- The parish church is little more than an extension of the
  country club: it does not enhance its parishioners' spiritual journey, it does not feed them spiritually, and it
  tends to think only of its own needs.

The complete list of reasons why people leave the Episcopal
Church is of course much longer, but each item illustrates how
internal circumstances and ever-deepening conflicts, when
blended with the bad-temperedness of this age, have eroded
Episcopal loyalties.

∞ Partisan Divisions

Whereas in the past the church was able to remain united despite
its diversity, today this is increasingly difficult. The manner in
which Christians are divided among themselves, especially Episcopalians, reflects the rifts that disfigure our society. Today the
zealots, who increasingly dominate all debates, are determined to
win at any price. The philosophical, social, and theological pre-
suppositions behind the issues separating us are now so far apart,
and competing factions have become so partisan, that we have
run out of solutions which might hold us together. Extremists on
one side encourage acts of ecclesiastical disobedience to assert
their views, while those on the other claim that the Episcopal
Church is already apostate. Division within the church has gone
beyond the shell-lobbing of the various single-issue groups
spawned during the last quarter-century.[14]

There is a determination among many in the church to use
political skills to maneuver toward one particular vision for the
future. For example, just as the church has settled down and is
coming to appreciate the 1979 *Book of Common Prayer,* lobbying

---

13. Both of these anxieties were fueled in the first part of 1996 by the Presiding
    Bishop's support of President Clinton's veto of legislation banning late and
    partial abortions, and by the Diocese of Newark's resolution to study the issue
    of voluntary euthanasia, seemingly putting a positive spin upon this practice.
14. See Richard Kew and Roger White, *New Millennium, New Church* (Cambridge,
    MA: Cowley, 1992), pp. 123-133.

is already going on for liturgies that will endorse a new set of theological emphases and linguistic correctness. Meanwhile, disregarding Anglicanism's historic comprehensiveness, champions of women's ordination are determined to remove from the canons the "conscience clause" still protecting those with deep—and thoroughly Anglican—reservations. If this change passes the 1997 General Convention, "liberals" are likely to take reprisals against "conservatives" for the presentment against Bishop Righter with a presentment of their own. It seems that the middle ground has long since vanished. In the midst of all this we totally lose our perspective of what God has called us to be, and the unchurched are denied the proclamation of the gospel.

In times like this, when the whole culture is roiled by tectonic change, many Christians trapped in the middle of these increasingly nasty conflicts are saying, "A plague on all your houses." Some join the fray, many more depart; the majority become silent and isolated worshipers, shunning the antagonisms at all costs. Meanwhile, outsiders look on and shake their heads, wondering why anyone in his or her right mind would get involved in the church. In a survey of the unchurched one person is reported to have said, "Why should I get involved in the church? I have enough problems of my own!"

Our cherished Anglican comprehensiveness has caved in. What is happening in our church—and indeed in most denominations—reflects a no-holds-barred competition between radically different visions for the future. Even during the battles of the 1970s, we sought ways to help those on the losing side of ecclesiastical struggles to save face. Such civility is a thing of the past. Today some appear determined to go so far as humiliating adversaries, then running them out of town on a rail. This conflict-ridden "win at all costs" mindset is accelerating the Episcopal Church's institutional collapse.

Passionate debate is healthy, but when it turns nasty and resorts to character assassination, it is time for all parties to take a long look at themselves and ask fundamental questions about their Christian commitment. At this point in time we can still listen to the apostle Paul, who said of contentiousness among Christians, "You did not so learn Christ"—though most of us are likely to direct this admonition at our ideological opponents rather than apply it to ourselves!

∞ *Possible Ways Forward*

Things are changing so fast that a bewildering array of scenarios could become realities very quickly. At this time there are so many wild cards in play that all we can confidently predict is that whatever happens, the future shape of the Episcopal Church will be very different from the past. Several times in the course of writing we have gone back to modify the fictional scenario with which we began, to make it much less specific about Bishop Donatello-Scott and the nature of the diocese of 2015; we realized how much our earlier drafts underestimated the potential for change. As the church reorganizes itself, the truth really could be stranger than fiction—and infinitely more exciting.

As a Methodist and a distinguished church consultant, Lyle Schaller has seen how many denominations face the same dilemmas. His book *Tattered Trust* is subtitled *Is There Hope for Your Denomination?* because he recognizes that all of the older churches in America are at a "fork-in-the-road," and will be shaped by "decisions being made now [that] will be implemented in the years ahead."[15] He looks out across churches riven by competing factions and sees many of the same stand-offs, in which national budgets and pluralistic judicatories look increasing unrealistic. A United Methodist bishop, for example, confessed to us that issues of sexuality were read into every debate and resolution at their 1996 General Conference. Schaller suggests that denominations should stick to doing those things they are good at—like managing pension funds and providing support networks for congregations and judicatories—in order to have the flexibility to meet changing needs.

---

15. Schaller, *Tattered Trust*, p. 13.

What follows are three scenarios for the organizational future of the Episcopal Church. While the eventual reality may be very different from what we suggest here, many of the issues raised by each of these models are likely to figure in the debate and decision-making. As we look at these models we need to ask if we should develop denominational structures and then build new strategies around them, or whether we should allow new strategies to emerge and then develop structures which will enable them to flourish.

∞ Scenario One: Turning the Episcopal Church into a Mixture of Geographical and Non-Geographical Dioceses

Schaller, who sees the same immense polity problems in the Methodist conference system as we often have in our dioceses, suggests a radical shaking out of the structure. He expects greater autonomy, and asks "Why shouldn't those at the grassroots be trusted to come up with radical alternatives?"

One option is non-geographical judicatories, since a geographical diocese divided by excessive theological and agenda diversity has become incapable of fulfilling its fundamental mission. While some might choose to continue as a part of a geographical entity, others will affiliate with congregations with whom they share commonality: be it ethnic, generational, theological, or ministry priorities. This opens a number of political cans of worms, not least the questions of size, how congregations decide which diocese to join, how such a transition might be managed, how relationships might be terminated, and so forth. But non-geographical judicatories would certainly allow a denomination to remain relatively intact and live with its pluralistic breadth.

The idea is intriguing, and we have been pondering how this might work in the Episcopal Church. The Episcopal Church has long since abandoned the approach, rooted in Europe's antiquity, of territorial parishes, and there is no biblical mandate for a pastoral unit to be geographical. Given our diversity and the options communications technology allows, is there any reason that the dioceses of the twenty-first century must be contained within geographical boundaries?

There are hundreds of parishes that feel isolated and disenfranchised, partly because their diocese is at a different place on the spectrum than they are. This is particularly true of traditional catholics, evangelicals, and charismatics, but it is also true of more "liberal" parishes in more "conservative" dioceses. The Diocese of Navajoland, for example, is evidence that the Episcopal Church believes there are circumstances when pastoral care for ethnic concerns overrides geographical considerations. Such an approach has been taken in other parts of the Anglican world as well: the Church of New Zealand, for example, has several dioceses specifically for Maori peoples overlaid on the seven geographical dioceses. Why not other distinctives in addition to ethnicity?

This scenario would certainly require a wholesale redrawing of boundaries, but in many places this is already long overdue. There is bound to be raucous protest for a variety of reasons. Some will argue on theological and ecclesiological grounds, others out of unwillingness to change, and still others because this is likely to pry power and funds from them. One prime objection will be that this change would be tantamount to the church's fragmentation, or "Balkanization." Maybe, but the reality is that we are already well down the road to *de facto* Balkanization. We further conjecture that a little Balkanization in the midst of the wholesale reordering of the churches is far better than involving ourselves in the post-modern equivalent of the vicious religious conflicts that accompanied the first Reformation. Such fights would absorb time, energy, and resources at a moment when millions are spiritually starving and seeking sustenance. If mission is to be our primary objective in the years ahead, there is greater likelihood that networked non-geographical dioceses with shared priorities could be an important part of the mix. While such a radical reworking should not be undertaken lightly, and many objections may be valid, something new ought to be tried.

∞ *Scenario Two: Turn the Episcopal Church into a Network of*
   Autonomous Provinces of the Anglican Communion

Another suggestion is to split the Episcopal Church up regionally. One idea, which originated with Kevin Martin of the Diocese of Texas, is to permit each of our nine regional provinces to become an autonomous province of the Anglican Communion. Given that present provincial alignments are already by and large non-functional, however, it might be better to draw new regional boundaries. In the process, it would probably be realistic to whittle them down from nine regional to five new autonomous provinces. While none are uniform in theology or philosophy of ministry, there are diverse regional variants which provide a large measure of commonality. The notion also honors the geographic principle for the diocese that the church catholic has maintained for nearly two millennia.

In such a scenario, there is nothing to prevent all kinds of shared ministry between dioceses and parishes in different provinces; neither is there any reason why clergy should not continue to move as freely as at present. England has two provinces and clergy move between Canterbury and York with ease. Furthermore, neither of us had major problems moving to this Anglican province, one of us from the Province of Canterbury and the other from the Province of York.

Sociological geographers have codified the "national identities" that make up the United States. Joel Garreau, for example, argued in 1981 that North America was, in reality, nine distinct social and racial entities that can be described as "nations."[16] While there are countless similarities among Americans, there are also regional differences, in many cases distinctives that are more stark than those between sovereign nations in other parts of the

---

16. Joel Garreau, *The Nine Nations of North America* (New York: Avon Books, 1981).

world. Each requires a radically different approach to ministry. The challenges facing dioceses in "MexAmerica," for example, are often utterly dissimilar to those confronting the church in the "Old South" or in New England. If each province had autonomy, then it could begin to develop the environment in which dioceses and congregations could pursue a distinctive regional strategy. There would be nothing to prevent cooperation between provinces over common approaches to mission, or even sending personnel and resources to help. The Church Pension Fund, Church Hymnal Corporation, and so forth, would continue to serve these provinces, unless for some reason, a province decided to opt out and go its own way.

There are numerous advantages to organizing in this way, but also some important questions. The first is whether the rest of the Anglican Communion would countenance such a change, although many existing provinces in the Communion are far smaller than any of these five potential new provinces. A second would depend on a majority of dioceses or the existing regional provinces being willing to realign. Furthermore, what is there to stop a newly-formed autonomous province from developing non-geographical dioceses which gather congregations from outside their region, or to agree upon an ecumenical merger with a denomination which has congregations in a different province? These are serious questions, yet they should not prevent us from exploring this second scenario.

∽ Scenario Three: Fragmentation, Schism, Recoalescing

The problem with the ideas outlined above is that each would take time to engineer—and time is growing short. There are deep fissures, and patience is wearing thin in many places. Although in some ways the report being developed by the Standing Commission on Structure for the 1997 General Convention—a tentative interim issue of which was published just as we were completing this book—is heading in the right direction, it is mistaken in thinking that time is on our side. Early on the commission notes that "the basic structures of this Church have served well the Church and its mission and ministry for over two centuries. There is clearly no need to hastily abandon the fundamental components."[17] This assumption reflects either a lack of awareness or a naiveté about the reality. The report reveals a reluctance to press the issues to their logical conclusion.

As we travel and talk to people around the country, we have come to see their frustration and impatience as the defining emotions. Many are ready to take matters into their own hands. In the previous generation, beginning with the uncanonical ordination of women in Philadelphia in 1974, impatience had a way of winning the day. With each passing week, fewer are willing to wait while standing commissions dance a stately gavotte and while new ideas are lost in the machinations of General Convention. A similar impatience is also burgeoning within the life of other Christian traditions. We are far closer to the front edge of several generations of structural reconfiguration than many imagine. It only takes one respected denomination—like our own, for instance—to start unravelling, and permission is given for the same thing to happen elsewhere.

Although the event had not been planned to follow the publication of the opinions on the Righter Presentment, in June 1996 a cross-section of laity, bishops, priests, and deacons who consider themselves to be part of the theologically "orthodox" wings of the church met in Northbrook, Illinois, to form the American Anglican Council. The Council is still in flux as to the form it will take, but for those who feel that their biblical and catholic sensibilities have been compromised within the Episcopal Church it is an attempt to find new ways to "be church." The AAC could very well turn into "a church within the Church." The members of this coalition fear that historical orthodoxy is under fire, that the Episcopal Church is reneging on its commitment to classic Anglicanism, and that, although committed to remaining part of the church, it is conceivable that at some point in the future it might be impossible for them to remain within its structures.

---

17. Report of Standing Commission on Structure (June 25, 1996).

At about the same time, a radically different group gathered at Trinity Cathedral in Columbia, South Carolina, to discuss "Out of the Whirlwind: Claiming a Vision for Progressive Christianity." Ninety participants who consider themselves part of the "progressive" wing of the church talked about "transforming an institution with a nineteen-hundred-year history of oppression and exclusion." From the opening sermon by a retired bishop who suggested the time had come to reformulate the Nicene Creed, through an emphasis on "gay, lesbian, bisexual, and transgender issues" and inclusive-language liturgies, to a final call for acts of "civil disobedience and ecclesiastical disobedience" on behalf of homosexual ordinations and same-sex unions, it was clear their goal was to foment a radical theological and ethical revolution within the church.

These very different gatherings illustrate how dry the tinder is, and how little it would take for a spark to ignite a prairie fire. Furthermore, the actions of such groups could presage a change in the relationship between the Episcopal Church and the rest of the Anglican Communion. When the episcopal court hearing the Righter Presentment opined that the Episcopal Church at this point had no declared theology on homosexuality, the pronouncement was greeted with dismay in many parts of the world. Both African dioceses and a South American province condemned this opinion, and more radical action could be taken in many corners of a communion in which the western churches are a shrinking minority, should the 1997 General Convention vote to ordain non-celibate homosexuals.

In a relatively short time the lid could well blow off the pressure cooker which is the Episcopal Church. As we have suggested already, we could still muddle through, but the likelihood diminishes daily. Such forced restructuring would begin with fragmentation, while bishops and other leaders desperately attempt to stem the tide. But there comes a point where critical mass carries all before it, and given today's fissures, this point could be reached fairly quickly.

The initial fragmentation would probably take place at the more conservative end of the ecclesiastical spectrum. There, those who believe they are conserving the historic continuity of Anglicanism have considerable affinity with non-canonical Anglican bodies such as the Reformed, Charismatic, and Evangelical Episcopal Churches. It is likely that arrangements for fellowship, intercommunion, and even full mutual recognition could follow.

One of the key reasons for the extraordinary success of newly-founded denominations like the Charismatic and Evangelical Episcopal Churches is that many are attracted to Anglicanism's richness and rootedness in tradition, but they are unwilling to affiliate with the Episcopal Church because they believe it could lead them to compromise their principles. There is enough circumstantial evidence to suggest that if a new, smaller, more conservative, totally reconfigured Anglican entity were to rise phoenix-like from the ashes of the old Episcopal Church, there would be many congregations from burgeoning nondenominational and independent movements who would decide in increasing numbers to affiliate with it.

In the process a new kind of Anglicanism would be born, out of which different kinds of ecclesiastical structures would evolve. Many provinces of the Anglican Communion would recognize this newly-developing Anglicanism in the United States even if formal Communion-wide recognition would, at least for a time, be withheld. We are already seeing Christians beginning to realign themselves along non-traditional lines. Is it possible that this emerging Anglicanism would be enriched by newcomers bringing treasures from, say, Methodism, Presbyterianism, Pentecostalism, and the rapidly growing independent churches, as well as Orthodoxy and Catholicism?

While such a transformation is taking place at one end of the ecclesiastical spectrum, something similar could occur at the other end. It could be that if the ordination of non-celibate homosexuals and the blessing of same-sex unions is approved, thereby alienating more conservative members of the church, it could lead to the fragmentation of yet another layer of moderate churchgoers who find that on these particular points the church has gone too far off-course for them to stay.

Meanwhile, the residual Episcopal Church (as well as this newly-formed style of Anglicanism) could be mired in financial problems. If the denomination is feeling an economic chill now, soon it may experience a genuine arctic breeze! It is highly likely that many endowed funds and properties would be frozen, while endless legal battles over to whom they rightfully belong would rage. Unless some process is negotiated to enable each side to emerge without too much loss of face over tangible assets, the church will be impoverished and animosities deepened by the struggles surrounding ownership—and these would take place at every level of church life, from parishes and dioceses to trust funds administered by the national church.

Furthermore, when churches split they set back their ministry for decades. The last major fragmentation of American denominations was in the 1920s, when several Protestant churches divided between "fundamentalists" and "modernists." Not only did the "modernists" never recover lost momentum, the "fundamentalist" conservative churches took several generations to put a new infrastructure in place. Only in the last twenty years have they been belatedly making the sort of impact that might have occurred earlier had there not been such turmoil.

However you look at it, division and schism would be devastating. Individuals and parishes would emerge scarred and damaged—some irreparably. Many such congregations would eventually be among those 100,000 to 150,000 American congregations that will die in the next half century. Ministries would be stillborn, intense animosities would obliterate the love of Christ, and resources would be diverted. The question is, do we want this to happen, and is it even preventable by this point in time? We have to raise the storm warning for those in our midst determined to champion their own particular cause, no matter the cost. Sadly, all victories in conflicts like this tend to Pyrric, the moment of "victory" really being defeat in a different guise, deflecting the church from its real mission.

The picture is far more complex and fraught that we have been able to demonstrate here. We have no doubt missed twists and turns which could make the road ahead even more hazardous. However, as puzzling as all this is, there is little doubt that God is "re-forming" the church for a new millennium. While the Holy Spirit could ultimately bring glory to God out of any shattered wreckage we might create, the road back to ecclesiastical health would be long, complicated, and not without considerable pain. There is evidence that the rediscovered spirituality of our age is full of opportunity for Christian mission, but if the Episcopal Church is not prepared to deal with the issues which we have started to outline, it is likely to become the church equivalent of Nash, Studebaker, or Rambler early in the coming century.

SUMMARY

- Any restructuring we do has to bear in mind that the local congregation is the frontline of the church's mission.

- The "Christendom paradigm" has passed. The future structure of the church will be radically different.

- The ecclesiastical landscape is changing as massive church migrations take place and new denominations come into being.

- Loyalties are changing as Episcopalians depart for a variety of reasons.

- The Episcopal Church has become a coalition of polarized and competing factions, some of which are determined their own agenda will win at all costs.

- One scenario for the future might be a mixture of geographical and non-geographical dioceses.

- A second scenario for the future might be a network of autonomous Anglican provinces within the United States.

- A third scenario for the future might be to come through fragmentation and schism to ecclesiastical realignment.

- The financial, spiritual, and emotional cost of division would be enormous.

- The result of fragmentation is most likely that we will be a "has-been" church.

QUESTIONS FOR DISCUSSION

- What signs do you see that the local congregation is on the frontline of mission?

- Do you see any evidence of denominational dissatisfaction and realignment? If so, what is behind it? If not, do you think it could happen?

- Look at Mark 2:20-22. What is Jesus teaching the church when he talks about new wineskins?

- Episcopalians have always been loyal to their church. Is there a point at which we should turn our backs on loyalty to a particular denomination?

- Look at the merits of each of the three scenarios for the future. Are there other scenarios you can imagine?

- Is the fragmentation of the Episcopal Church and other denominations inevitable?

- What suggestions do you have to prevent the Episcopal Church from becoming a "has-been"?

11

What Business are We In?

We met a good friend for lunch recently. Inevitably, the progress we were making on this book came up in the conversation. The only work we needed to do on the manuscript was to tie up the loose ends, and to complete this final chapter. As we chatted, our friend, a priest, turned to the challenges he sees facing the Episcopal Church.

"You know," he began, "the Episcopal Church is a little like those great railroad barons of the last century. They had put in place a wonderful infrastructure, they had tons of money, they had enormous land holdings, but they had forgotten what business they were in." He paused to make sure he had our attention, then continued. "They thought their business was railroading, but in reality it was transportation. This meant that they missed the opportunity when cars came along, then again when the airlines took to the skies. The railroads have missed the opportunity to transport millions of people; today they mainly ship freight."

We nodded. Churches, like businesspeople, can get so carried away with themselves and their own importance that they do not keep asking—and seeking to answer—those fundamental questions which point to a healthy future. Our friend completed his illustration. "I love this church," he said movingly. "It's been my family's church for generations. I love all that it stands for. But like those old railroad barons we have forgotten that our business is making new Christians; instead, we've committed ourselves to making Anglicans! Just look at all the resources, real estate, and roots that we have, but we've forgotten how to make Christians out of people—that's the key."

This man should know—he leads one of the most remarkable parishes in the United States today. He knew that if they had just set out to breed a new generation of Episcopalians, they would not have become a center for evangelism and exciting ministry, but would have remained the respectable little fellowship that the congregation had been in previous generations.

While this book has outlined the trends buffeting our world and the currents sweeping along the life of our church, the real focus has been our response to all that is happening—which should be mission and evangelism. The future of the Episcopal Church is dependent on us being able to birth and nurture generation after generation of new Christians. It is dependent on us getting beyond self-serving myopia and the survival mentality, and seeing that there is a huge world out there that is spiritually hungry and eager to hear about Christ—as long as we tell people in words they understand and in a style which makes sense to them.

If we are in the business of proclaiming Christ and making new Christians, all that we are and do must be seen in terms of bringing in God's Kingdom upon earth in the person of Jesus Christ. There are no limits to what is possible; neither are there any limits to what God might ask us to do. However, if we are determined merely to make Anglicans, our vision will be small and our goals extraordinarily limited. If our primary aim is to induct people into *this* church, and not much more, then we are likely to see our ministry in terms of preserving old liturgies, old buildings, old music, old structures, and old ways of doing things. There is not necessarily anything bad in what we have inherited, but too often we have turned these things into idols, and as such they have kept us from seeing the enormous opportunities which God has spread out before us.

This book has been about beginning the transition away from merely making Anglicans, toward the breathtaking business of making Christians and taking the message of salvation into all the world. There are good reasons why the churches are being battered by waves of creative destruction. Yesterday's solutions now seldom work, and simply doing better what we have done in the past is just about the best way to fail in the future. To paraphrase the philosopher Alfred North Whitehead, familiar patterns fade, familiar solutions fail, and familiar options are being foreclosed on us.

We have intentionally said little about the seemingly endless procession of controversies that have confused the once orderly life of the church, not because they are unimportant, but because for the most part they are mere symptoms of the seismic shifts taking place everywhere—especially under our own feet! Conflicts like these are little more than local skirmishes in a far larger battle. Like most others, we see no easy solution to these seemingly intractable disputes which loom before us. This reality is raising frustration levels, but the conflict could very well be part of the process whereby all Christian churches are being reshaped.

What is happening in the church is not taking place in a vacuum, but is a religious and spiritual reflection of a more radical reformation of global society and the reinventing of almost all institutions. Indeed, what is happening spiritually could be undergirding all these societal changes, rather than the other way round.

There are, sadly, bound to be casualties in every revolution, including the one which is enveloping the church. However, if we persist in concentrating on the minutiae we will fail to see the big picture, and then will miss how God is at work in our midst. Out of the crucible into which we have now been cast will come a people who have been tested, and who will hopefully be more attentive to God's call to mission.

Rabbi Edwin Friedman spoke at the Shaping Our Future symposium in St. Louis in 1993, as an outsider looking in on the Episcopal Church. He told us that the whole of our society has been "stuck" for a while, and that the church is not alone as it flounders toward a way forward. The picture we have painted might seem disturbing, but we sense that God is lifting us from the morass of the present confusion and malaise and equipping us to venture forth into this brand new era. But no reformation ever occurs overnight. The seeds of this new beginning have been planted: now are we going to let them grow and bear fruit, or will we attempt to crush them?

By 2015 a new kind of church could well have started to emerge, phoenix-like, from the ashes. Most of our culture's institutions are being reinvented around us, and the same rebuilding process is being forced upon the church's life. Some are escaping into 1950s-style ecclesiastical cocoons of their own making, but this is not the way forward if we are to be the missionary people of God in the future. When the rebuilding process is over, North American Anglicanism will look and feel very different—but we believe that a critical mass of local Episcopal parishes will once again be making Christians and not just Anglicans.

However, a warning must be sounded. The story of the Christian faith is littered with examples of churches that once prospered but which are now little more than ruins to be visited by curious tourists. The great Nestorian Church of the East, for example, was probably driven by the missionary imperative more strongly than almost any in the early centuries of Christian history. At one point it stretched from the Mediterranean to western China and boasted more than two hundred fifty dioceses. Today it is hardly a whisper of its former self, with only a few pockets of believers here and there across a predominantly non-Christian landscape.

The Nestorian church, like the churches of North Africa of the same period, assumed its future was guaranteed. But no church, including the Episcopal Church, has any God-given right to continue to exist if it does not fulfill the mission to which God has called it. The writing is on the wall for most of the old-line denominations in general and the Episcopal Church in particular. We estimate that no more than ten to fifteen percent of all our parishes take mission and evangelism seriously; the vast majority of the remainder are in a maintenance mode at best, and are more likely to be obsessed with issues of survival than proclamation.

Meanwhile, healthy developments—like the urge to plant new churches—are being stymied by either the misdirection of resources or the failure to see that the multiplication of new congregations eventually brings great blessing to the whole, as well as glory to God. We heard recently of a deanery of congregations which was discouraging the planting of a new parish in their locality despite the fact that the whole metropolitan region in which they are situated estimates that it could double in population during the next decade. Unfortunately, this is not an isolated example of resistance and lack of vision. With up to ninety percent of church members focused on themselves, their own needs, and their survival, it is obvious that if we are to begin to fulfill our potential, a mammoth redirection needs to get underway. And this needs to be happening *now*!

Despite such discouraging resistance, a new church really is being born. It is our prayer that the church which looks out upon the new millennium will have a fresher face, will be more confident of God's call to mission, and perhaps more eager for selfless servant ministry. As we offer our prayers and seek God's will, we must ask ourselves "What business is our church in?"

Epilogue

A licia Donatello-Scott wearily trudged up the stairs, as she did each New Year's morning when her husband disappeared into his study. He had spoken movingly of his vision for the future at the midnight prayer service at St. Timothy's, and now, despite her urgings, he had gone off to begin his journal for the year 2016. She entered the bedroom, turned down the covers of the bed, and began preparing herself for a short night's rest—she was exhausted. As she sat before the mirror brushing her hair, Alicia marveled at the progress they saw every time they went back to St. Timothy's.

St. Timothy's continued to go from strength to strength, in marked contrast to a number of the congregations which had surrounded the church when they first moved to that part of the country. Unable to make the transitions necessary for effective ministry in the first quarter of the new century, a good few parishes had slowly shrivelled, until it had been necessary for Barry, in the early years of his episcopate, to close their doors forever. This had been profoundly painful for the few remaining faithful members of those congregations and it had taken a intense toll on her husband's spiritual and mental health.

Yet the counterbalance had been the steady progress of the many new congregations that had been planted since the turn of the century, some of whom were now attaining a considerable degree of spiritual maturity and missionary vision. Often led by visionary and prayerful teams which included both clergy and laity, they seemed able to tap the extraordinary gifts and resources which were pent up inside their membership. It was also striking how much younger the average age of these parish members was, and she had heard Barry mention that the new church members had considerably reduced the median age of Episcopalians in the whole diocese.

As she climbed into bed and turned out the light, knowing that it could be at least an hour before her husband came upstairs, Alicia shot an arrow of thanks to God for all that had happened and the quiet power of the Holy Spirit in their midst. She drifted off to sleep in the early hours of that New Year's morning wondering what God might have in store in the very exciting future she had heard her husband outline that evening.

Downstairs, the nib of her husband's pen moved fluently across the page as he attempted to reproduce in his diary some of the things he had said at the midnight service. As his stream of thoughts began drying up, Barry looked across the room toward his desk. On the shelf beside it were some of the many resources upon which he drew when leading worship, but he had been formed in the faith by the words of the old Prayer Book of 1979. Getting up from his comfortable chair, he walked over and pulled from the shelf the now tattered copy that had been presented to him when he had become rector of St. Timothy's almost twenty years before.

Sitting down again, he flicked through the familiar pages, occasionally pausing and reading something before going on. Finally he found the prayer for the mission of the church he was looking for toward the end of the book. He set the Prayer Book beside his journal, then prayed the prayer as he copied it. It seemed to him to sum up and surround the transformation that was taking place in his diocese and in many other corners of the church. It also expressed many of his hopes and longings for the years ahead:

Everliving God, whose will it is that all should come to you through your Son Jesus Christ: Inspire our witness to him, that all may know the power of his forgiveness and the hope of his resurrection; who lives and reigns with you and the Holy Spirit, one God, now and for ever. Amen.

Barry closed his Prayer Book and journal, thanking God for the many opportunities for service there had been in 2015 and eagerly looking forward to all that lay ahead.

Bibliography

Barna, George. *The Frog in the Kettle*. Ventura, CA: Regal Books, 1990.

Barna, George. *Evangelism that Works*. Ventura, CA: Regal Books, 1995.

Bosch, David J. *Transforming Mission*. Maryknoll, NY: Orbis Books, 1991.

Campolo, Tony. *Can the Mainline Denominations Make a Comeback?* Valley Forge, PA: Judson Press, 1995.

Drucker, Peter F. *Post-Capitalist Society*. New York: Harper Business, 1993.

Easum, William. *Dancing with Dinosaurs*. Nashville: Abingdon Press, 1993.

Easum, William. *Sacred Cows Make Gourmet Burgers*. Nashville: Abingdon Press, 1995.

Fenhagen, James C. *Ministry for a New Time*. Washington, D.C.: The Alban Institute, 1995.

France, R.T., and Alister McGrath. *Evangelical Anglicans: Their Role and Influence in the Church Today*. London: SPCK, 1993.

Fries, Heinrich and Karl Rahner. *Unity of Churches: An Actual Possibility*. Philadelphia: Fortress Press, 1988.

Garrett, Laurie. *Coming Plague*. New York: Penguin Books, 1995.

George, Carl. *The Coming Church Revolution: Empowering Church Leaders for the Future*. Grand Rapids, MI: Fleming Revell, 1994.

Green, Michael, and Alister McGrath. *Springboard for Faith.* London: Hodder and Stoughton, 1993.

Guinness, Os. *The American Hour.* New York: The Free Press, 1993.

Guinness, Os, and John Seel, eds. *No God but God.* Chicago: Moody Press, 1992.

Hadaway, C. Kirk, and David A. Roozen. *Rerouting the Protestant Mainstream.* Nashville: Abingdon Press, 1995.

Howe, Neil, and Bill Strauss. *13th Generation: Abort, Retry, Ignore, Fail?* New York: Vintage Books, 1993.

Hunter, George G., III. *How to Reach Secular People.* Nashville: Abingdon Press, 1992.

Hunter, George G., III. *Church for the Unchurched.* Nashville: Abingdon Press, 1996.

Huntingdon, Samuel P. "The Clash of Civilizations?" *Foreign Affairs* (Summer 1993).

Kaplan, Robert D. *The Ends of the Earth: A Journey at the Dawn of the 21st Century.* New York: Random House, 1996.

Kennedy, Paul. *Preparing for the Twenty-First Century.* New York: Random House, 1993.

Kew, Richard, and Cyril Okorocha. *Vision Bearers.* Harrisburg, PA: Morehouse Publishing, 1996.

Kew, Richard, and Roger White. Articles published in *The Living Church* from March 1995 to May 1996.

Kew, Richard, and Roger White. *New Millennium, New Church.* Cambridge, MA: Cowley Publications, 1992.

Kew, Richard, and Roger White. *Venturing into the New Millennium.* Solon, OH: Latimer Press, 1994.

Keck, Leander. *The Church Confident.* Nashville: Abingdon Press, 1993.

Lipnack, Jessica, and Jeffrey Stamps. *The Age of Networks.* Essex Junction, VT: Omneo, 1994.

Manchester, William. *A World Lit Only By Fire.* Boston: Little Brown, 1992.

McGrath, Alister. *Reformation Thought: An Introduction.* Oxford: Basil Blackwell, 1988.

McGrath, Alister. *Evangelicalism and the Future of World Christianity.* London: Hodder and Stoughton, 1994.

McGrath, Alister. *A Passion for Truth.* Downers Grove, IL: Inter-Varsity Press, 1996.

Mead, Loren. *The Once and Future Church.* Washington, D.C.: The Alban Institute, 1991.

Mead, Loren. *Transforming Congregations for the Future.* Washington, D.C.: The Alban Institute, 1994.

Messer, Donald E. *Calling Church and Seminary into the 21st Century.* Nashville: Abingdon Press, 1995.

Naisbitt, John. *Megatrends Asia.* New York: Simon and Shuster, 1996.

Newbigin, Lesslie. *The Gospel in a Pluralistic Society.* London: SPCK, 1989.

Newbigin, Lesslie. *Unfinished Agenda.* London: SPCK and Grand Rapids, MI: Wm. B. Eerdman and Company, 1985.

Oden, Thomas C. *Requiem: A Lament in Three Parts.* Nashville: Abingdon Press, 1995.

Peterson, Eugene H. *Under the Unpredictable Plant.* Grand Rapids, MI: Wm. B. Eerdman and Company, 1992.

Popcorn, Faith. *The Popcorn Report.* New York: HarperBusiness, 1992.

Schaller, Lyle E. *It's a Different World!* Nashville: Abingdon Press, 1987.

Schaller, Lyle E. *The New Reformation.* Nashville: Abingdon Press, 1995.

Schaller, Lyle E. *Tattered Trust: Is There Hope for Your Denomination?* Nashville: Abingdon Press, 1996.

Shawchuck, Norman, and Gustave Rath. *Benchmarks of Quality in the Church.* Nashville: Abingdon Press, 1994.

Sine, Tom. *The Mustard Seed Conspiracy.* Dallas: Word Books, 1981.

Sine, Tom. *Wild Hope.* Dallas: Word Books, 1991.

Sine, Tom. *Cease Fire.* Grand Rapids, MI: Wm. B. Eerdman & Company, 1995.

Snow, John. *The Impossible Vocation: Ministry in the Mean Time.* Cambridge, MA: Cowley Publications, 1988.

Snyder, Howard A. *EarthCurrents: The Struggle for the World's Soul.* Nashville: Abingdon Press, 1995.

Sweet, Leonard. *FaithQuakes.* Nashville: Abingdon, 1994.

Toffler, Alvin and Heidi. *Creating a New Civilization.* Atlanta: Turner Publishing, 1995.

Travis, Stephen. *All Things to All People: Mission Beyond 2000.* Nottingham, England: St. John's Theological College, 1995.

Wells, David F. *No Place for Truth.* Grand Rapids, MI: Wm. B. Eerdman & Company, 1993.

Wright, N. Thomas. *Bringing the Church to the World.* Minneapolis: Bethany House, 1992.

Wuthnow, Robert. *Sharing the Journey: Support Groups and America's New Quest for Community.* New York: The Free Press, 1994.

Ministry Resources

Continuing the Debate

Toward 2015: A Church Odyssey is our contribution to a much larger debate going on in churches all over the United States and in many other parts of the world. The debate is only just getting underway, and will continue for several generations. This book is therefore designed to stimulate others to join in the quest to build a church whose passion it is to proclaim Jesus Christ.

To help foster the debate:

- We have established a home page on the World Wide Web at http://www.episcopalian.org/2015/. The page will be a source of new data, resources, and ideas, and will enable us to interact with one another, develop ideas, and pray together for our mission into the new millennium.

- We will be leading conferences built around this book in various places in the years ahead, beginning with the conference "2015: A Church Odyssey" in June 1997 at the Kanuga Conference Center in North Carolina (phone 704-692-9136).

- We are available to conduct conferences and workshops, and to consult with parishes, dioceses, and organizations seeking to grapple creatively with the future:

The Rt. Revd. Roger J. White
The Diocese of Milwaukee
804 E. Juneau Avenue
Milwaukee, WI 53202
Phone: 414-272-3028
Fax: 414-272-7790
E-mail: RJWhite787@aol.com

The Revd. Richard Kew
P. O. Box 2806
Murfreesboro, TN 37133-2806
Phone: 615-849-1354
Fax: 615-848-9143
E-mail: RichardKew@aol.com
or RichardKew@XC.org

We hope that you will want to get involved in these endeavors, and that you will share with us your thoughts and ideas so we can move together into what could be a very exciting tomorrow.

Other Resources for Ministry

The Alban Institute

4550 Montgomery Ave, Suite 433, Bethesda, MD 20814
Phone: 301-718-4407

For many years the Alban Institute has worked in the area of congregational dynamics. It publishes a most helpful journal, *Congregations.*

The Alpha Course

Holy Trinity Church
Brompton Road, London SW7 1JA, England
or Truro Episcopal Church
10520 Main Street, Fairfax, VA 22030
Phone: 703-273-8686; Fax: 703-591-0737

The Alpha Course is a nonthreatening evangelistic program designed to reach out in a warm and sensitive way to the unchurched. It began at Holy Trinity Church in London.

The Anglican Fellowship of Prayer
P. O. Box 31, Orlando, FL 32802
Phone: 407-438-3166; Fax: 407-856-1578
http://www.afp.org/
The Anglican Fellowship of Prayer has sought to encourage and equip the life of prayer in various parts of the Anglican Communion for more than half a century. Part of Richard Kew's vocation is to work as Director of Ministry of AFP.

Anglican Frontier Missions
P. O. Box 18024, Richmond, VA 23226
Phone: 804-355-8468
E-Mail: AFM@XC.org
http://www.episcopalian.org
Working with Christians of many other traditions, AFM seeks to develop strategies and reach out with the gospel to the least evangelized peoples in the world. AFM is particularly committed to using modern communications for world evangelization, and to developing non-residential missionaries.

Building Parishes around Small Groups
One of the most successful proponents of this in the Episcopal Church has been Trinity Church, Carrollton, Texas. For information and resources contact:
The Revd. Dr. Bill Atwood
Trinity Church
1415 Halsey Way, Suite 320; Carrollton, TX 75007-4455
Phone: 214-245-3400; Fax: 214-245-3472
E-Mail: EUNBill@aol.com

The Cornerstone Project
The Episcopal Church Foundation
815 Second Avenue, New York, NY 10017
Phone: 212-697-2858
The Cornerstone Project attempts to address the spirituality of both parishes and clergy.

Diocese of Texas Congregational Development Office

The Revd. Canon Kevin Martin is a creative and informed thinker about the interface of the local church with the changes occuring in the wider church and the world. He can be reached at:

Episcopal Diocese of Texas

P. O. Box 2247, Austin, TX 78768-2247

Phone: 512-478-0580; Fax: 512-478-5615

E-Mail: CanonKevin@aol.com

Episcopal Church Missionary Community

P. O. Box 278, Ambridge, PA 15003-0278

Phone: 412-266-2810; Fax: 412-266-6773

E-Mail: 102350.3234@compuserve.com

http://www.episcopalian.org

Founded in 1974, ECMC has pioneered world mission education in the Episcopal Church and has encouraged people to give and to go. It was involved in the formation of the Stanway Institute for Evangelism and Mission, part of Trinity Episcopal School for Ministry. ECMC is a good place for people to begin, when they start exploring global ministry.

Global Evangelization Movement Research

GEM Research

1301 N. Hamilton, Suite 209, Richmond, VA 23230

E-Mail: GEM@XC.org

http://www.goshen.net/gem

Directed by the Revd. Dr. David B. Barrett, editor of the *World Christian Encyclopedia*, GEM has one of the most significant ongoing research programs into the future shape of the world and of world Christianity anywhere. The new edition of the encyclopedia will be published by the Oxford University Press in 1997 both in book and CD-ROM form. Their bi-monthly *AD 2025 Global Monitor* is the most thorough regular review of the changing world scene and least evangelized peoples available.

Leadership Network
P.O. Box 9100, Tyler, TX 75711-9100
Phone: 800-765-5323; 903-561-0437 (outside the USA)
Fax: 903-561-9361

An interdenominational meeting point for those concerned for visionary Christian leadership, the Leadership Network is a treasury of resources, ideas, meeting-places, and publications. They are doing a great deal to help congregations and their leaders move forward dynamically into the new millennium. *NetFax* is a regular fax publication of the Leadership Network which is available free.

North American Missionary Society
P.O. Box 1457, Pawleys Island, SC 29585
Phone: 800-441-NAMS, 803-237-1525; Fax: 803-237-1958
E-Mail: NAMSHQ@aol.com
http://www.episcopalian.org

This Episcopal home mission society whose focus is church planting is a major resource being developed within the church. Its General Secretary is the Revd. Dr. Jon Shuler.

Open Theological College
Information about this novel approach to theological education being pioneered by a consortium of theological seminaries in Britain can be obtained from:
St. John's Theological College
Chilwell Lane
Bramcote, Nottingham HG9 3DS, England
Phone: 0160 222 5046; Fax: 0161 222 0134

Princeton Religion Research Center
47 Hulfish Street
P. O. Box 389, Princeton, NJ 08542
Phone: 609-921-8112; Fax: 609-924-0228

From their annual report, *Religion in America,* to their ten-times-a-year newsletter, *Emerging Trends,* the resources produced by

George H. Gallup, Jr., and his team are an excellent starting point for understanding the part religion plays in our culture.

Reaching Generation X

Bill Haley, Director of Outreach and ministry to Generation X at the Falls Church, Falls Church, Virginia, is one of the most thoughtful and provocative proponents of ministry to this age group. He may be reached at:

Mr. William R. L. Haley
The Falls Church
115 E. Fairfax Street, Falls Church, VA 22046
Phone: 703-532-7600; Fax: 703-532-3321
E-Mail: 75537.1464@Compuserve.com

Religion Watch

P. O. Box 652, North Bellmore, NY 11710
Phone: 516-785-6765
E-Mail: relwatch@aol.com

Religion Watch is a monthly newsletter committed to monitoring trends in contemporary religion. It is probably just about the best "early warning system" available for those who want to be on top of the circumstances shaping the churches and other religions, from both within and without.

Russian Ministry Network

P. O. Box 2806, Murfreesboro, TN 37133-2806
Phone: 615-849-1354; Fax: 615-848-9143;
E-Mail: RichardKew@XC.org or RichardKew@aol.com
http://www.episcopalian.org

The Russian Ministry Network provides coordination between grassroots ministries in the Episcopal Church and the work of Russian Orthodoxy. Arranging parish partnerships, the exchange of data and resources, and the building of person-to-person relationships, it provides an environment in which local mission initiatives in cooperation with the Russians can prosper.

SOMA (Sharing of Ministries Abroad)
5290 Saratoga Lane, Woodbridge, VA 22193
Phone: 703-878-7667; Fax: 703-878-7015
E-Mail: SOMAUSA@aol.com

SOMA is part of a worldwide network of mission agencies in the renewal tradition, committed to equipping the church to fulfill the Great Commission, providing short-term mission opportunities for Episcopalians to go in teams to dioceses around the world. Teams always go at the invitation of the local bishop.

South American Missionary Society
P. O. Box 399, Ambridge, PA 15003
Phone: 412-266-0669; Fax: 412-266-0297
E-mail: SAMS@episcopalian.org
http://www.episcopalian.org

The oldest of the voluntary sending missionary agencies in the Episcopal Church, SAMS has played a significant role in reworking world mission in the Episcopal Church and exploring new church planting methods under the leadership of its Executive Director, the Revd. Canon Tom Prichard.

Cowley Publications is a ministry of the Society of St. John the Evangelist, a religious community for men in the Episcopal Church. Emerging from the Society's tradition of prayer, theological reflection, and diversity of mission, the press is centered in the rich heritage of the Anglican Communion.

Cowley Publications seeks to provide books, audio cassettes, and other resources for the ongoing theological exploration and spiritual development of the Episcopal Church and others in the body of Christ. To this end, it is dedicated to developing a new generation of theological writers, encouraging them to produce timely, creative, and stimulating publications of excellence, and making these publications available widely, reaching both clergy and lay persons.